PRINCE2 Agile™: An Implementation Pocket Guide

Step-by-step advice for every project type

PRINCE2 Agile™: An Implementation Pocket Guide

Step-by-step advice for every project type

JAMIE LYNN COOKE

IT Governance Publishing

Every possible effort has been made to ensure that the information contained in this book is accurate at the time of going to press, and the publisher and the author cannot accept responsibility for any errors or omissions, however caused. Any opinions expressed in this book are those of the author, not the publisher. Websites identified are for reference only, not endorsement, and any website visits are at the reader's own risk. No responsibility for loss or damage occasioned to any person acting, or refraining from action, as a result of the material in this publication can be accepted by the publisher or the author.

Apart from any fair dealing for the purposes of research or private study, or criticism or review, as permitted under the Copyright, Designs and Patents Act 1988, this publication may only be reproduced, stored or transmitted, in any form, or by any means, with the prior permission in writing of the publisher or, in the case of reprographic reproduction, in accordance with the terms of licences issued by the Copyright Licensing Agency. Enquiries concerning reproduction outside those terms should be sent to the publisher at the following address:

IT Governance Publishing
IT Governance Limited
Unit 3, Clive Court
Bartholomew's Walk
Cambridgeshire Business Park
Ely, Cambridgeshire
CB7 4EA
United Kingdom

www.itgovernance.co.uk

© Jamie Lynn Cooke 2016

The author has asserted the rights of the author under the Copyright, Designs and Patents Act, 1988, to be identified as the author of this work.

PRINCE2 Agile™ is a trade mark of AXELOS
PRINCE2® is a registered trade mark of AXELOS

First published in the United Kingdom in 2016
by IT Governance Publishing.

ISBN 978-1-84928-807-1

DEDICATION

To my father, Alan, for teaching me the value of analysis and the power of persistence.

FOREWORD

At first, I thought PRINCE2 Agile™ was an oxymoron. How could it be possible to combine the flexibility that Agile brings with the structure and approach of PRINCE2®? Agile focuses on the issues on the left of the Agile Manifesto[1] – the importance of people working collaboratively to produce a working product in small iterations whilst responding to in-flight changes. I associate PRINCE2 with the other, right-hand side of the Agile Manifesto – with managing projects using processes and tools, sticking to a plan and providing comprehensive governance documentation. Moreover, Agile is not a project governance tool, and PRINCE2 does not provide an approach for getting the business change, IT service, or other product actually built, delivered, and implemented. How could these seemingly contradictory approaches work together?

Understanding this dichotomy is critical for my work. Many of my clients (and similar organizations) want to use Agile methods, but equally need to demonstrate extremely high standards of governance and other managerial control. This is particularly true of organizations in the government and banking sectors, many of whom already use PRINCE2 for their projects. These organizations have a great need for implementing changes quickly and effectively, but a requirement to still maintain sufficient governance to satisfy Boards, regulators and financial markets. This is where PRINCE2 Agile is ideal. It provides a logical and flexible framework for those organizations wishing to develop a realistic balance between the forces of Agile and governance. In my opinion, the PRINCE2 Agile approach is far better than many of the other cumbersome attempts to place project management and governance controls on top of Agile methods.

---

[1] See *www.agilemanifesto.org*.

Foreword

PRINCE2 Agile™: An *Implementation Pocket Guide* provides a very useful explanation of the PRINCE2 Agile framework and guidance on how to implement it – especially for those who need a readily available reference source to supplement the official PRINCE2 Agile guide. This book provides practical advice on how to adopt – and adapt – the PRINCE2 Agile approach to the needs of your organization's project – whatever its size or complexity. Many of the suggestions in this book can equally be applied to existing PRINCE2 organizations and to those without formal governance structures, to organizations who have delivered traditional waterfall projects as well as those experienced in Agile methods. I will be adding the guide to my toolkit and would urge you to do so also.

Christopher Wright BSc(Hons.), CPFA, CISA, MBCS, MAPM, CSM

Agile Governance and Audit Author, Consultant, Trainer and Coach

Director, Wright-CandA Consulting Ltd

PREFACE

There was a time when business planning was an *annual activity*, with key decision-makers getting together before the start of each fiscal year, identifying the corporate objectives for the upcoming year, establishing the corresponding annual budgets, and documenting these details in an annual report.

This approach worked (reasonably) well in a world where market conditions were relatively stable, technology innovations were slow and infrequent, competition was a known quantity, and staff were in it for the long haul. That is not today's corporate world.

In today's ever-changing, fast-moving, global-reaching marketplace, the key to maintaining your competitive advantage, keeping your products and services relevant, and retaining your customers is *responsiveness* – being in a position to *adapt* the work that the organization is doing *at any time* to align with the most current market, competitive, and corporate information available.

The paradox is that, even though the business climate has changed, the basic principles of fiscal responsibility, due diligence, and corporate governance need to remain in order for senior management to ensure that operating costs are being expended on those activities that will generate the most significant business value for the organization. It is the same requirement that existed in the world where executives could make key decisions on an annual basis, get monthly status reports, and revisit them the following year to see the outcomes; but we no longer live in that world.

The executive management of an organization in today's marketplace still needs to maintain responsibility for corporate governance even when the landscape is changing on a monthly, weekly, or even daily basis. They face a constant struggle to balance the need to support a viable business case and ensure

Preface

fiscal responsibility in managing overhead costs with the need to be responsive to ongoing changes in technology, market conditions, and resources.

This is why PRINCE2 Agile™ is ideal for today's corporate world. It combines the governance, due diligence, and accountability that senior management requires with the responsiveness and flexibility that project delivery teams need to do their jobs most effectively:

PRINCE2 Agile enables businesses to become more competitive by focusing on delivery as well as project direction and management.[2]

Interestingly, PRINCE2 Agile does more than provide the framework that allows executives, project delivery teams, and business stakeholders to work towards a shared goal; it also provides a previously unheard-of level of communication, information sharing, and, most importantly, trust.

Executives can know the project status any time that they require without asking for specially created reports. This means that they can confidently leave the project delivery team to get the job done, knowing that, if there are significant changes, the PRINCE2 Agile exception-reporting structure will advise them.

It also means that delivery team members are *empowered* to do the work that is required with the full support of management – and without having to put their work on hold (and shift their focus) to write lengthy status reports or wait for management approvals.

If your organization has already invested time and resources in establishing a PRINCE2® framework, the transition to

---

[2] *Taking Agile to PRINCE2*, Raconteur (2015), http://raconteur.net/business/taking-agile-to-prince2.

Preface

PRINCE2 Agile is, in many respects, an extension of the procedures and practices that staff currently use – although it may require a shift in their mindset. (See *Chapter 4: Five Keys to PRINCE2 Agile Success*.)

If you do not have an existing governance framework, this is an opportunity to invest in a model that leverages the proven best practices of PRINCE2 and the responsive, business-value driven productivity of Agile methods.

PRINCE2 Agile™: An Implementation Pocket Guide is structured to enable you to successfully implement PRINCE2 Agile in a range of corporate scenarios, including:

- PRINCE2 organizations that want to implement PRINCE2 Agile to get the benefits of Agile methods.
- PRINCE2 organizations that want to merge their existing Agile project work into the combined PRINCE2 Agile framework.
- PRINCE2 organizations that want to transition the next stage of their existing waterfall projects into the combined PRINCE2 Agile framework.
- Organizations with no existing governance structure or project delivery method that want to implement PRINCE2 Agile as an integrated governance and project delivery framework.
- Organizations that currently use Agile methods with no governance framework that want to implement PRINCE2 Agile to provide greater alignment between their Agile work and corporate objectives.

This book is intended for anyone who is impacted by a PRINCE2 Agile project, either directly as a project team member or indirectly as an affected business area, such as customer service, quality assurance, and project administration.

Most importantly, the guidance in this book adheres to one of the core principles of PRINCE2 Agile by providing *flexible* options in each scenario to allow you to implement the processes, tools and structures that are best suited to the specific needs of your project – and your organization.

ABOUT THE AUTHOR

Jamie Lynn Cooke has 25 years' experience as a senior business analyst, project manager, and solutions consultant, working with more than 130 public and private sector organizations throughout Australia, Canada, and the United States.

She is the author of *Agile Productivity Unleashed: Proven Approaches for Achieving Real Productivity Gains in Any Organization*, a book written specifically to explain Agile methods in nontechnical business terms to managers and executives outside the IT industry; *Agile: An Executive Guide: Real Results from IT budgets*, which gives IT executives the tools and strategies needed for bottom-line business decisions on using Agile methods; *Everything You Want to Know about Agile: How to Get Agile Results in a Less-than-Agile Organization*, which gives readers strategies for aligning Agile work within the reporting, budgeting, staffing, and governance constraints of their organization; and *The Power of the Agile Business Analyst: 30 Surprising Ways a Business Analyst Can Add Value to Your Agile Development Team*, which details 30 core activities that Agile business analysts can undertake to ensure that Agile development teams deliver the highest possible business-value solution for the organization.

Jamie is a well-regarded speaker on both business and technology topics, most recently presenting on issues such as "Getting Management and Business User Support for Using Agile" and "When Is Agile Not the Answer?" at the Business Process Modelling world conference in Brisbane, Australia and at the AgileCanberra professional forums.

Jamie is a Certified Scrum Product Owner and Certified ScrumMaster who has been working hands-on with Agile methods since 2003, and has researched hundreds of books and articles on Agile topics. She is a signatory to the Agile Manifesto, has attended numerous Agile seminars, and has

About the Author

worked with prominent consultants to promote Agile methods to organizations worldwide.

She has also been actively involved in a range of successful PRINCE2 projects in her work with the Australian Government.

Jamie has a Bachelor of Science in Engineering Psychology (Human Factors Engineering) from Tufts University in Medford, Massachusetts, and a Graduate Certificate in e-Business/Business Informatics from the University of Canberra in Australia.

ACKNOWLEDGEMENTS

Thank you to Keith Richards and his collaborators for producing an excellent guide to PRINCE2 Agile, and to AXELOS for allowing portions of the guide to be used in this publication.

Continued thanks to the pioneers and thought leaders of the Agile world, most notably Kent Beck, Martin Fowler, Alistair Cockburn, Jeff Sutherland, Mike Cohn, Ken Schwaber, and Jim Highsmith, for their passionate work in developing and refining Agile methods over the past two decades.

Thanks also to the small and large organizations worldwide that have shared their Agile experiences, including Nokia Siemens Networks™, Yahoo!™, Google™, Microsoft®, and BT™.

Special thanks to Vicki Utting of IT Governance Publishing and Stacey Czarnowski of Studio B for their ongoing support and excellent advice. Thanks also to Christopher Wright for his honest and insightful Foreword.

Many thanks, as well, to the people who taught me the most about the strategies of the business world over the past 25 years, especially Roland Scornavacca, Tony Robey, and Peter Walsh; to Rowan Bunning for being an unending source of Agile knowledge; and to the writers and teachers who inspired me, particularly Richard Leonard for his amazing ability to encourage writers with his humor and enthusiasm.[3]

Finally, my eternal gratitude to my parents, my US family, my Australian family, and my friends, most especially Susan,

---

[3] See Richard Leonard's website at richardleonard.net.

Acknowledgements

Michele, Elissa, Janice, and Linda, for continuing to be my sanity check in this world. Most of all, thank you to my husband, David, for 24 years of love and laughter.

CONTENTS

Introduction 1
Chapter 1: Overview of PRINCE2 9
Chapter 2: Overview of Agile 17
Chapter 3: Overview of PRINCE2 Agile 23
Chapter 4: Five Keys to PRINCE2 Agile Success 43
Chapter 5: Moving from PRINCE2 to PRINCE2 Agile ...51
Chapter 6: Merging Existing PRINCE2 and Agile Methods 71
Chapter 7: Moving an Existing Waterfall Project to PRINCE2 Agile 75
Chapter 8: Implementing PRINCE2 Agile with No Existing Framework 79
Chapter 9: Moving from Agile to PRINCE2 Agile 81
Chapter 10: Further Expansion of PRINCE2 Agile 83
Bibliography 85
ITG Resources 91

INTRODUCTION

In a world where an organization's responsiveness to change can be the difference between its long-term survival and its short-term departure, it is no surprise that organizations are moving toward more *agile* ways of doing business. Changes in technology, market conditions, external suppliers, and internal staff all contribute to the need for organizations to be positioned to *adapt* and *evolve* ongoing work to reflect the most current information available:

Organizations that adopt agile behaviors and techniques stand to gain from early delivery of more projects … faster returns on their investment … a competitive edge.[4]

The challenge for these organizations is in establishing an environment that supports responsiveness to ongoing changes *without* jeopardizing the need to ensure that corporate funds are being used effectively and delivering their intended business value.

PRINCE2 Agile is the ideal coupling of governance and responsiveness in a rapidly changing marketplace. It gives senior management the level of control and access to critical project information that it needs for confident ongoing decision-making. It also empowers the project team to deliver adaptable, high business-value outputs within the allocated project timeframe and budget.

For organizations who currently utilize PRINCE2 methods, the incorporation of Agile methods in a PRINCE2 Agile framework provides an unprecedented level of flexibility, responsiveness,

---

[4] *Taking Agile to PRINCE2*, Raconteur (2015),
http://raconteur.net/business/taking-agile-to-prince2.

and transparency to project delivery that gives the Project Board the ongoing evidence it needs to confidently progress (or to strategically limit) project work.

For organizations who currently utilize both PRINCE2 and Agile methods *independently* (i.e. without an integrated approach), implementing PRINCE2 Agile provides an opportunity to bring together these methods into a cohesive framework and leverage the benefits of both. The combined governance of PRINCE2 Agile better aligns existing Agile project work to corporate objectives and provides the project delivery team with greater management visibility and support. It also provides senior management with greater visibility into project progress, more confidence in the value of project outputs, and greater flexibility to adapt ongoing project work to meet changing corporate and market conditions.

For organizations in an environment with *no existing framework*, PRINCE2 Agile provides an unparalleled combination of corporate governance and flexible delivery to support the needs of both senior management and the project delivery team members.

Most importantly, for all organizations, PRINCE2 Agile provides a shared framework for communication, status updates and issue resolution that focuses the entire team on continually delivering high business-value outcomes. It gives senior management exceptional insight into project work and ongoing confirmation of business-value generation. It also allows project delivery team members to better understand – and appreciate – the overarching business drivers that the project work is based on, and the correlation between business-value generation and continued project funding.

As part of this shared framework, PRINCE2 Agile project teams use high-value communication tools, such as *information radiators*, to allow Project Board members to know the status of project work at any time, without waiting for a highlight report, checkpoint report, end stage report, or exception report. (This also reduces overheads for the project manager, and saves the project delivery team from stopping their work – and shifting their focus – to create ad hoc status reports.)

The successful implementation of PRINCE2 Agile requires far more than an agreed set of procedures and documents for the project team – it requires a shared vision, a collaborative mindset, and an open and honest working environment. Although the Project Board, project manager, and project delivery team members all have different responsibilities, they have a *shared objective* to deliver valuable outcomes in the PRINCE2 Agile framework.

How to use this guide

The key to successfully implementing PRINCE2 Agile is in understanding how it brings together PRINCE2 and Agile best practices into a cohesive framework, and how to adapt that framework to meet your needs. This guide is specifically structured to provide you with the core information that you need to understand how PRINCE2 Agile works, and implementation guidelines specific to the needs of your organization and your projects.[5]

The first three chapters of this guide describe how PRINCE2 and Agile methods each work independently, and how PRINCE2 Agile brings them together into a cohesive framework:

---

[5] The AXELOS Official PRINCE2 Agile Guide provides a complete and comprehensive description of PRINCE2 Agile, including all of the information that you will need for PRINCE2 Agile certification. It is strongly recommended that you read this book in conjunction with the AXELOS official guide, not in lieu of it. It is also recommended that anyone who interested in implementing PRINCE2 Agile go to the AXELOS website (*www.axelos.com/qualifications/prince2-qualifications/prince2-agile*) for information about formal training and certification.

Introduction

Chapter 1: Overview of PRINCE2 describes the key elements of the PRINCE2 governance framework.

Chapter 2: Overview of Agile describes the most common Agile methods that are used for project delivery.

Chapter 3: Overview of PRINCE2 Agile describes how these two approaches are combined into a unified project governance and delivery framework with a focus on the benefits that this integrated approach provides.

Chapter 4: Five Keys to PRINCE2 Agile Success identifies the five most important factors for you to consider when implementing PRINCE2 Agile.

To implement PRINCE2 Agile most effectively in your organization, it is essential for you to use your current governance, project management, and project delivery frameworks as the baseline for moving forward. The next five chapters of this book provide you with guidelines specific to the needs of your organization:

- *Chapter 5: Moving from PRINCE2 to PRINCE2 Agile*
- *Chapter 6: Merging Existing PRINCE2 and Agile Methods*
- *Chapter 7: Moving an Existing Waterfall Project to PRINCE2 Agile*
- *Chapter 8: Implementing PRINCE2 Agile with No Existing Framework*
- *Chapter 9: Moving from Agile to PRINCE2 Agile*

Figure 1 shows you how each of these implementation chapters aligns with your specific circumstances, and guides you on the most appropriate chapter(s) for you to focus on in your reading.

Introduction

	If you are an existing PRINCE2 organization running waterfall projects exclusively:	If you are an existing PRINCE2 organization running both waterfall and Agile projects:	If your organization has no existing governance framework and you are running waterfall projects exclusively:	If your organization has no existing governance framework and you are running both waterfall and Agile projects:
Chapter 5: Moving From PRINCE2 to PRINCE2 Agile	Provides step-by-step guidelines for PRINCE2 organizations that want to transition their projects to PRINCE2 Agile	Start with this chapter		
Chapter 6: Merging Existing PRINCE2 and Agile Methods	Offers additional guidance for organizations that want to transition their projects to PRINCE2 Agile and leverage the Agile methods that their project teams are current using	Start with this chapter		

Chapter 7: Moving an Existing Waterfall Project to PRINCE2 Agile	Provides step-by-step guidance for PRINCE2 organizations that want to transition their active waterfall projects to PRINCE2 Agile	Read this chapter for additional information on transitioning your existing waterfall projects to PRINCE2 Agile	
Chapter 8: Implementing PRINCE2 Agile with No Existing Framework	Gives organizations with no existing governance framework a starting point for implementing a PRINCE2 Agile framework to provide both governance and effective project delivery	Read this chapter for additional information on transitioning your existing waterfall projects to PRINCE2 Agile	Start with this chapter
Chapter 9: Moving From Agile to PRINCE2 Agile	Guides organizations who are actively using Agile methods on incorporating PRINCE2 Agile as an integrated governance framework		Start with this chapter

Figure 1: Selecting the most suitable PRINCE2 Agile implementation approach for your organization

Introduction

When you have finished reading the implementation chapter(s) that are suited to your needs, *Chapter 10: Further Expansion of PRINCE2 Agile* offers an approach for expanding your use of PRINCE2 Agile beyond project work.

The guidelines in this book, when used in conjunction with the detailed information in the AXELOS official PRINCE2 Agile guide,[6] provide you with realistic and achievable approaches for implementing a PRINCE2 Agile framework that can consistently deliver responsive, high business-value project outcomes.

---

[6] PRINCE2 Agile: *www.axelos.com/store/book/prince2-agile*.

CHAPTER 1: OVERVIEW OF PRINCE2

PRINCE2 (PRojects IN Controlled Environments) is a project management and governance framework that is used in more than 150 countries.[7] It provides senior management with ongoing assurance that their funded projects are generating the expected level of business value.

The PRINCE2 framework has the flexibility to be applied to projects of any type, size, duration, complexity, and scope, and is applicable to both Information Technology (IT) and non-IT projects.

PRINCE2 is based on the understanding that well-managed projects need:

- to *start* with a justified business case and an organized plan for delivering the identified business value.
- to *progress* in a way that enables the project delivery team to generate the required outputs with ongoing assurance to senior management that:
  o work is progressing
  o changes, issues, and risks are being managed
  o agreed timelines, budgets, and quality metrics are being achieved and
  o the business case for the project work continues to be justified.
- to *complete* the project with confirmation of the achieved business value, documented records of the project work (and closure), and feedback to the organization on lessons learned to benefit future projects.

---

[7] Foreword, *PRINCE2 Agile*, Keith Richards, AXELOS (2015): *www.axelos.com/store/book/prince2-agile*.

Chapter 1: Overview of PRINCE2

The PRINCE2 framework achieves this with an *integrated approach* of:[8]

Seven principles that guide all of the project work:

1. *Continued business justification* – is there a justifiable reason for starting the project that will remain consistent throughout its duration?
2. *Learning from experience* – PRINCE2 project teams should continually seek and draw on lessons learned from previous work.
3. *Defined roles and responsibilities* – the PRINCE2 project team should have a clear organizational structure and involve the right people in the right tasks.
4. *Management by stages* – PRINCE2 projects should be planned, monitored, and controlled on a stage-by-stage basis.
5. *Manage by exception* – PRINCE2 projects should have defined tolerances for each project objective to establish limits of delegated authority.
6. *A focus on products* – PRINCE2 projects focus on the product definition, delivery, and quality requirements.
7. *Tailoring to suit the project environment* – PRINCE2 is tailored to suit the project's environment, size, complexity, importance, capability, and risk.[9]

Seven themes of project management disciplines that need to be enforced throughout the project lifecycle:

---

[8] As described on the AXELOS Official PRINCE2 website at *www.axelos.com/best-practice-solutions/prince2/what-is-prince2*.
[9] Those readers who are familiar with Agile methods will see the alignment between PRINCE2 principles, such as Learn from Experience, and proven Agile practices.

Chapter 1: Overview of PRINCE2

1. *Business case*: What value would delivering the project bring to the organization?
2. *Organization*: How will the project team's individual roles and responsibilities be defined in order for them to effectively manage the project?
3. *Quality*: What quality requirements and measures are there and how will the project deliver them?
4. *Plans*: What steps are required to develop the plans and PRINCE2 techniques that should be used?
5. *Risk*: How will project management address the uncertainties in its plans and the project environment?
6. *Change* – How will project management assess and act on unforeseen issues or requests for change?
7. *Progress*: How will the ongoing viability and performance of the plans determine how (and whether) the project should proceed?[10]

Seven processes that comprise the full project lifecycle with detailed checklists of recommendations for each process:

1. *Starting up* a project.
2. *Directing* a project.
3. *Initiating* a project.
4. *Controlling* a stage.
5. *Managing product delivery*.
6. *Managing stage boundaries*.
7. *Closing* a project.

All of these are adaptable to suit any project environment.

---

[10] Those readers who are familiar with Agile methods will also see the alignment between PRINCE2 themes, such as Managing Quality and Risk, and proven Agile practices.

Chapter 1: Overview of PRINCE2

The PRINCE2 framework also defines specific project roles and responsibilities that are necessary to implement these principles, themes, and processes effectively, specifically:

- The *Project Board*, a group that is responsible for the overarching management of the project and ensuring that the project is continuing to deliver its intended business value for the organization. Minimally, the Project Board comprises three key participants:
  o The *Executive*, who represents the senior management interests of the organization and has the ultimate decision-making responsibility for the project.
  o The *Senior User(s)*, who represent the target audience that will be using the outputs from the project work and are responsible for making key decisions regarding the capabilities that the project team delivers.
  o The *Senior Supplier(s)*, who represent the internal or external team that is delivering the required outputs. Where work is being undertaken by multiple teams, e.g. an internal development team and an external software vendor, the Senior Supplier role may be filled by a key representative from each team.

  Other Project Board members are included as required to represent key functions across the organization, e.g. Quality Assurance, Customer Support.

- The *Project Manager*, who is responsible for the project delivery in accordance with the terms established by the Project Board, including allocating work; providing status updates; managing issues and risks; monitoring time, budget, scope, benefit, and quality tolerances; and raising exceptions.

There are other roles identified in PRINCE2, e.g. the team manager. These will be elaborated upon further in the PRINCE2 Agile implementation sections of this book.

In addition to the principles, themes, processes, and roles described, PRINCE2 identifies a number of project artifacts that need to be developed to authorize the project to begin and

Chapter 1: Overview of PRINCE2

to ensure effective ongoing project management, including the *project brief*, the *project initiation documentation (PID)*, the *project product description*, the *benefits review plan*, *stage plans*, *highlight reports*, *checkpoint reports*, *exception reports*, the *configuration item record*, the *issue register*, and the *risk register*. These will also be elaborated upon in the implementation sections.

To ensure that PRINCE2 is executed effectively, there is a structured PRINCE2 qualification scheme that provides globally recognized confirmation of three levels of PRINCE2 knowledge: Foundation, Practitioner, and Professional.[11]

Figure 2 provides an overview of the PRINCE2 project governance structure, including the relationship between the Project Board, the project manager and the project delivery team.

---

[11] See *www.axelos.com/qualifications/prince2-qualifications/prince2-agile*.

Chapter 1: Overview of PRINCE2

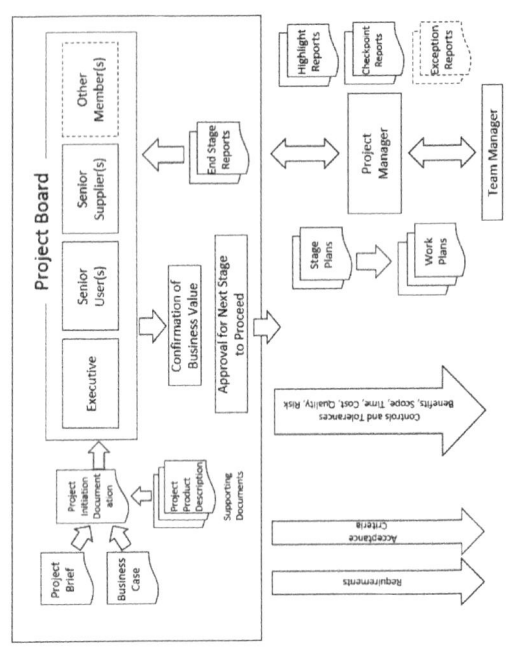

Chapter 1: Overview of PRINCE2

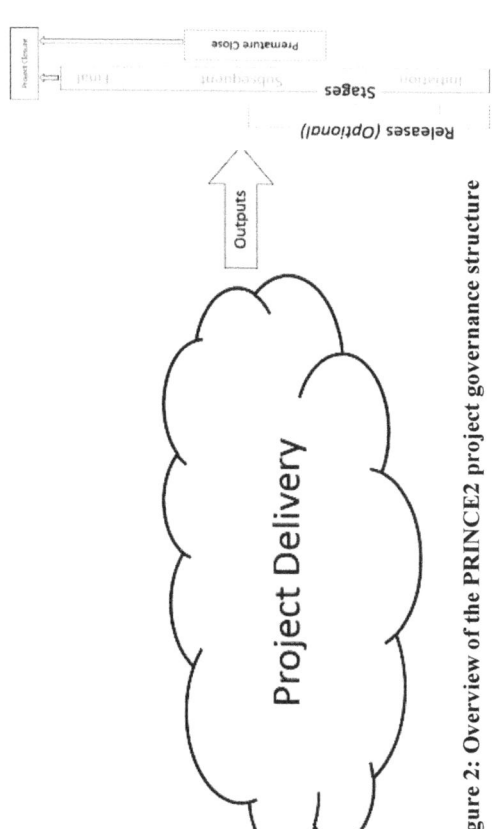

Figure 2: Overview of the PRINCE2 project governance structure

Chapter 1: Overview of PRINCE2

In reviewing this diagram, it is important to note the *cloud* that represents the project delivery team and the delivery process in PRINCE2. The PRINCE2 framework provides the expectations for *what* the project team will deliver, *when* it will be delivered, to what *level of quality*, and at what *cost*; it does not, however, specify *how* these required outputs are developed. That is the responsibility of the project delivery team under the guidance of the project manager.

The flexibility in delivery of PRINCE2 allows it to be applicable across a broad range of project types, durations, sizes, and levels of complexity. This flexibility is also the reason why PRINCE2 can readily incorporate, and integrate with, each of the Agile methods described in the following chapter.

Further detail about PRINCE2 and the PRINCE2 qualification is provided on the official PRINCE2 website at *www.axelos.com/best-practice-solutions/prince2*, with additional resources on PRINCE2 provided in the *Bibliography*.

CHAPTER 2: OVERVIEW OF AGILE

"Agile" is a collective term for *adaptive management* methodologies (and practices) that have emerged over the past two decades to increase the relevance, quality, flexibility, and value of business solutions.[12] They are commonsense approaches for applying the finite resources of an organization to continuously deliver low-risk, high business-value outputs within allocated time and budget constraints.

For the IT industry, these approaches are used to address the problems that have historically plagued software development and service delivery activities, including budget overruns, missed deadlines, low-quality outputs, and dissatisfied users.

Although there is a broad range of Agile methods in the IT industry – from software development and project delivery approaches to strategies for software maintenance – all Agile methods share the same basic objectives:

- To replace upfront planning with incremental planning that adapts to the most current information available ("Apply, Inspect, Adapt").
- To minimize the impact of changing requirements by providing a low-overhead structure to accommodate variations to the originally identified requirements throughout the project.

---

[12] For those who follow this author's writing, some of the introductory material from Jamie Lynn Cooke, *The Power of the Agile Business Analyst: 30 Surprising Ways a Business Analyst Can Add Value to Your Agile Development Team* (IT Governance Publishing, 2013), has been adapted for use in this book, serving the same purpose as in the original.

Chapter 2: Overview of Agile

- To build in quality up front and then relentlessly confirm the integrity of the solution throughout the process.
- To address risks as early in the process as possible to reduce the potential for cost and time blowouts as the project progresses.
- To entrust and empower staff to continuously deliver high business-value outputs by allowing them to manage their capacity and self-organize their work.
- To provide frequent and continuous business value to the organization by focusing staff on regularly delivering the highest-priority features in the solution as fully functional, fully tested, production-ready (i.e. potentially releasable) capabilities.
- To encourage ongoing communication between the business areas and project team members to increase the relevance, usability, quality, and acceptance of delivered solutions.

The last two bullet points in this list cannot be emphasized enough. Where traditional waterfall software development projects focus on using extensive upfront documentation to detail user requirements before development work can even begin, Agile approaches rely on *shared communication* between the development team and the business users throughout the project, with the business users' highest-priority requested features regularly presented to them as *fully functional software* to confirm whether or not the delivered solution meets their requirements.

Figure 3 provides an overview of the Agile project delivery structure.

Chapter 2: Overview of Agile

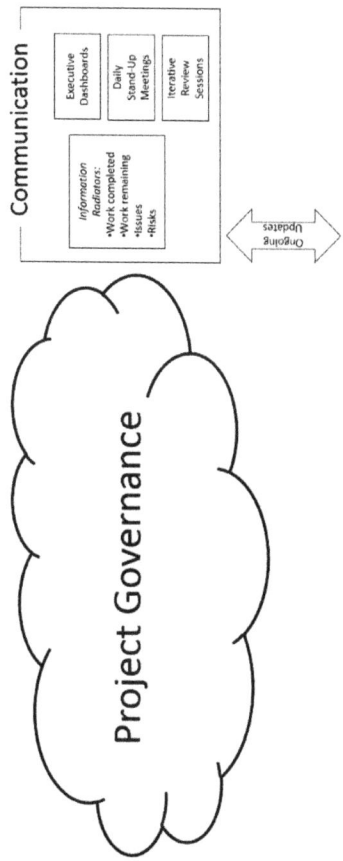

Chapter 2: Overview of Agile

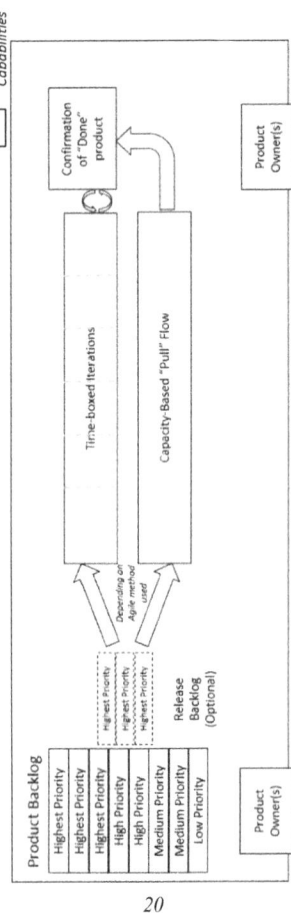

Figure 3: Overview of the Agile project delivery structure

In reviewing this diagram, it is important to note the *cloud* that represents project governance in Agile methods. These methods focus on how outputs are produced by the project delivery team to meet the highest-priority business requirements identified by the Product Manager. There is no standard governance or project management structure.

Some of the most common Agile methods include:

- Iterative strategies for managing software development projects, such as *Scrum*, *Dynamic Systems Development Method* (DSDM), *Feature-Driven Development*™ (FDD™), the *Rational Unified Process*® (RUP®), and the *Agile Unified Process* (AUP).

- Strategies for optimizing software development work, such as *eXtreme Programming* (XP™), and *Lean Development*.

- Strategies for managing software development projects, as well as maintenance and support activities, such as *Kanban* and *Scrumban*.

- Extensions of Agile methods to support large enterprise-wide teams and shared corporate objectives, such as the *Scaled Agile Framework*® (SAFe®), *Scrum of Scrums*, *Large-Scale Scrum Framework* (LeSS) and *Nexus*.

Chapter 2: Overview of Agile

These Agile methods have been (and continue to be) successfully used by thousands of organizations worldwide,[13] most notably in the United States, Europe, and Australia. Some of the more prominent organizations using Agile methods include Nokia Siemens Networks™,[14] Yahoo!™,[15] Google™,[16] Microsoft®,[17] BT™,[18] Bankwest™,[19] SunCorp™,[20] and Wells Fargo™.[21]

Further detail about Agile methods is provided in the *Bibliography*.

---

[13] As evidenced by the number of signatories to the Agile Manifesto (*www.agilemanifesto.org*) as of December 2015.

[14] P. Haapio, NokiaSiemens and Agile Development, JAOO (2008), *http://jaoo.dk/file?path=/jaoo-aarhus-2008/slides//PetriHaapio CanAGLobalCompany.pdf*.

[15] K. Mackie, Lessons from a Yahoo Scrum Rollout, (2008), *http://campustechnology.com/articles/2008/02/lessons-from-a-yahoo-scrum-rollout.aspx*.

[16] J. Sutherland, Scaling Scrum & Distributed Teams – Scrum Tuning: Lessons Learned at Google (2006): *www.youtube.com/watch?v=9y10Jvruc_Q*.

[17] D.K. Taft, Microsoft Lauds Scrum Method for Software Projects (2005), eweek.com/c/a/IT-Management/Microsoft-Lauds-Scrum-Method-for-Software-Projects.

[18] L. Meadows and S. Hanly, *Agile Coaching in British Telecom* (2006), *www.agilejournal.com/articles/columns/column-articles/144-agile-coaching-in-british-telecom*.

[19] D. Braue, Bankwest goes Agile: Project Time Slashed (2010), zdnet.com/bankwest-goes-Agile-project-time-slashed-1339306091.

[20] Suncorp goes Agile for 19k Desktop Integration Project (2008), *itnews.com.au/News/130927,suncorp-goes-Agile-for-19k-desktop-integrationproject.aspx*.

[21] E. Matta, Is Agile Development Only for Nerds? (2008), *http://radiowalker.wordpress.com/2008/10/07/is-Agile-development-only-for-nerds*.

CHAPTER 3: OVERVIEW OF PRINCE2 AGILE

PRINCE2 Agile is an *adaptive governance* method for project delivery which combines senior management's ongoing need for *business-value confirmation* and *due diligence* with the *empowerment* and *flexibility* that the project team needs to deliver the required outcomes.[22] It is the first extension module to the PRINCE2 method.[23]

PRINCE2 Agile combines PRINCE2 and Agile methods in a way that both

- maintains the integrity of the PRINCE2 principles, themes, processes, roles, and project artifacts described in *Chapter 1: Overview of PRINCE2* and
- delivers the efficiencies and core benefits of Agile methods described in *Chapter 2: Overview of Agile*.

Figure 4, from the AXELOS PRINCE2 Agile Official Guide, provides an overview of how these two approaches are combined into a cohesive framework.

---

[22] This section provides an overview of how the two approaches work together with a focus on the resulting benefits that organizations can achieve. Much more extensive detail on implementing PRINCE2 Agile is provided in the AXELOS official PRINCE2 Agile guide.
[23] Foreword, *PRINCE2 Agile*, Keith Richards, AXELOS (2015), www.axelos.com/store/book/prince2-agile.

Chapter 3: Overview of PRINCE2 Agile

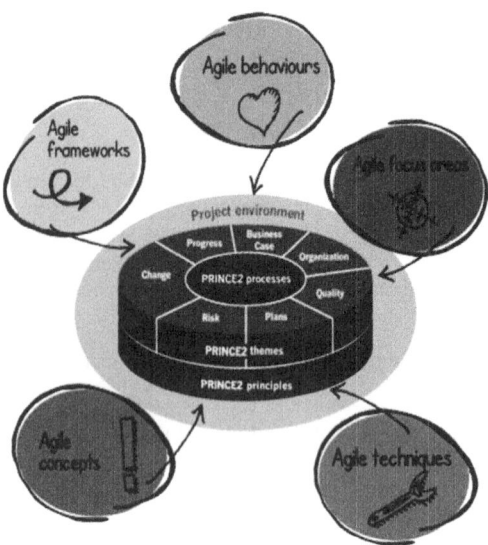

Figure 4: Tailoring PRINCE2 by blending in the Agile ingredients

Copyright © AXELOS Limited 2015. All rights reserved. Material is reproduced under licence from AXELOS

This section details how these two approaches work together cohesively, and the corresponding benefits that they can provide for your organization.

Why PRINCE2 Agile?

There is a broad range of benefits that can be achieved by implementing the PRINCE2 Agile framework for your projects, including:

Chapter 3: Overview of PRINCE2 Agile

- Increased rates of on-time and on-budget project delivery with project outcomes continually confirmed to meet business requirements.
- More cohesion between senior management and project delivery teams.
- Greater transparency and communication on ongoing project status for all stakeholders.
- Flexibility for you to adapt project work to meet changing requirements.
- The reliability of using a best-practices framework with formal training and globally recognized certification.

The specific benefits that your organization can achieve with PRINCE2 Agile will depend upon the methods that you are currently using for governance and project delivery.

For existing PRINCE2 organizations, the implementation of PRINCE2 Agile takes the value of project governance to the next level:

- Information on project status is continuously available to the Project Board and project manager as needed, instead of waiting for highlight reports, checkpoint reports, end stage reports, or raised exceptions.
- Project delivery teams are continually focused on delivering the highest business-value capabilities throughout the project.
- Project delivery teams are empowered to do the work that is required without significant reporting overheads or delays awaiting approvals.

For organizations who are implementing PRINCE2 Agile *without an existing governance framework*, these benefits are substantially more prominent, as the organization will gain both the immediate and ongoing advantages of having well-managed business outcomes with the high-productivity, value-driven focus of Agile methods at the same time.

Chapter 3: Overview of PRINCE2 Agile

PRINCE2 Agile achieves this integrated approach by establishing *baseline requirements* for projects to adhere to and then allowing the organization and the project team the *flexibility* to determine what roles, processes, and artifacts are needed specifically for each project. For this reason, PRINCE2 Agile is "Agile agnostic," supporting the Agile method(s) that are best suited to your organization and your projects.[24]

The following section describes how PRINCE2 Agile is able to provide this flexibility and deliver these benefits to your organization.

How does it work?

Figure 5 shows a summary of PRINCE2 Agile and how these methods work together.

---

[24] Where the AXELOS official guide incorporates a range of Agile methods, including Scrum, Kanban, and Lean.

Chapter 3: Overview of PRINCE2 Agile

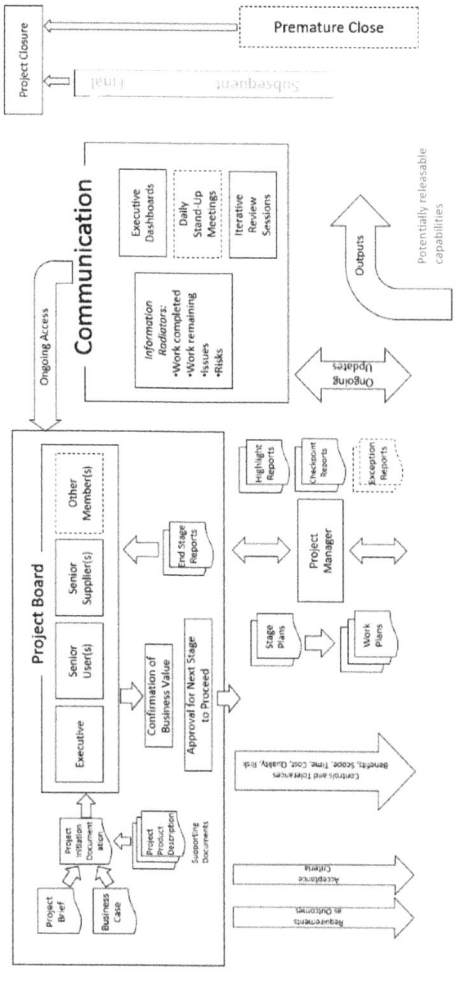

Chapter 3: Overview of PRINCE2 Agile

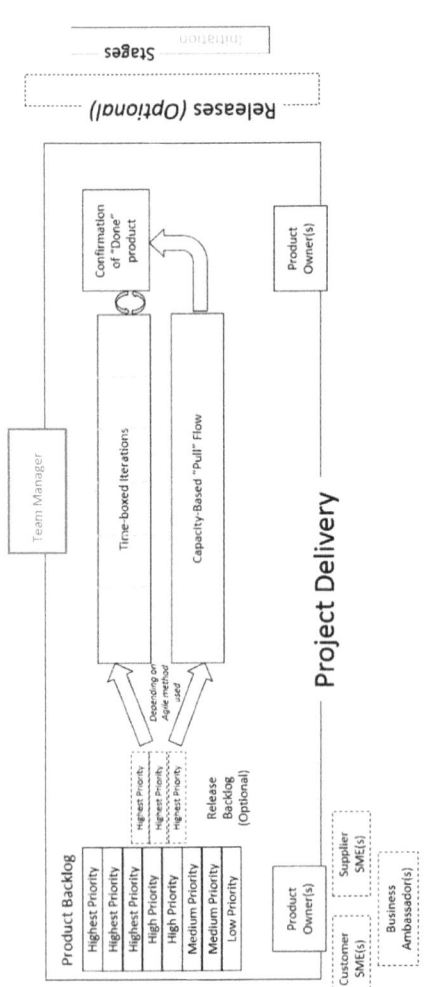

Figure 5: Overview of the PRINCE2 Agile integrated governance and project delivery framework

Chapter 3: Overview of PRINCE2 Agile

At the top of the diagram is the PRINCE2 project governance structure, with:

- Project work driven by a justified business case (the project brief) and a structured project delivery approach (the PID).
- Project oversight provided by the Project Board.
- Ongoing management and communication of project activities by the project manager using traditional PRINCE2 reporting tools.

At the bottom of the diagram is the selected Agile method for project delivery, with empowered teams undertaking priority-driven work using time-boxed iterations or capacity-based "pull" flows, along with high-value communication tools and frequent feedback channels.

In the middle of the diagram are the key touchpoints that allow PRINCE2 and Agile methods to work cohesively in the PRINCE2 Agile framework:

- **Requirements as Outcomes** and **Acceptance Criteria:** the capabilities that the solution is expected to deliver, described in a way that allows the product owner to make adjustments (i.e. "minor changes") and assess acceptability during each stage without significantly altering the expectations of the Project Board.
- **Controls** and **Tolerances:** the project variables that need to be managed as the project progresses (Benefits, Scope, Time, Cost, Quality, and Risk) in accordance with the acceptable levels identified by the Project Board. In PRINCE2 Agile, it is expected that some of these variables will be fixed (Time and Cost), some will have expected levels of flexibility (Scope and Quality), and some will be either fixed or flexible, depending on the nature of the project (Benefits and Risk). This distinction is further explained in the section below.
- **Outputs:** in PRINCE2 Agile, the most important measures of project progress and ongoing business value are the *potentially releasable capabilities* that the project delivery team produces in each management stage – and their

Chapter 3: Overview of PRINCE2 Agile

adherence to the agreed acceptance criteria (i.e. the quality criteria in PRINCE2). The business value that is produced in each stage is one of the most significant measures for the Project Board to determine the ongoing viability of the project and approve subsequent stages.

- **Issues and Risks:** as the project progresses, it is the responsibility of the entire project delivery team (not just the project manager) to identify potential issues and risks that could jeopardize the expected project outcomes.
- **Communication:** as high communication is a critical factor in the success of PRINCE2 Agile projects, this is an overarching, continuous, bidirectional connection between the Project Board and the project delivery team.

The outputs from the project delivery team are bundled for delivery in Iterations, Releases, and Stages, as required by each project.

The project manager and the team manager sit between Project Governance and Project Delivery, acting as a bridge between the Project Board and the project delivery team to identify required work, facilitate communication, escalate issues, and ensure compliance with the PRINCE2 Agile governance requirements. An important distinction in PRINCE2 Agile is that these are primarily *servant leadership* roles, where the project delivery team is responsible for managing their work, and the project manager and team manager are there to support the team's work and remove any obstacles to project delivery.

At first glance, it may appear that PRINCE2 Agile is essentially PRINCE2 and Agile working concurrently. It is true that there are many aspects of PRINCE2 Agile that retain features similar to those of each respective approach, but there are also significant differences that make this combined approach particularly powerful, starting with the *key principles* that govern PRINCE2 Agile work.

Chapter 3: Overview of PRINCE2 Agile

Key principles

PRINCE2 Agile fosters – and relies upon – an environment of:

- *Transparency*: ensuring that current project information is readily available to anyone in the organization with an interest in the work, including (but not limited to) the project delivery team, the project manager, the Project Board, and the intended business users.
- *Collaboration*: encouraging teams to work closely together towards a shared vision, to play an active role in project decisions, and to take responsibility for their committed outcomes.
- *Communication*: using high-value communication tools to provide transparency of information and to support ongoing collaboration.
- *Exploration*: empowering teams to investigate and trial potential solution options to confirm capabilities and to mitigate risks as early as possible. Note that this exploration work needs to be done with the Project Board's understanding that:
  o not all of the options explored will be viable.
  o parts of the investigation and trialing may require substantial rework, as well as the possibility of discarded work.
  o the results of the exploration work may require the original product requirements to be revisited and, in some cases, modified to establish a more achievable solution.
- *Self-organization*: empowering the project delivery team to allocate their work in a way that best utilizes the skills and strengths of the team members.
- *Accountability*: creating a shared ownership by all project team members for the successful delivery of the project outcomes.

For teams currently using Agile methods, these are core principles that already guide how the team interacts with each other and with the business representatives. In PRINCE2 Agile, these core principles are expanded upon to include everybody

Chapter 3: Overview of PRINCE2 Agile

involved in the project, from development team members to senior executives.

In addition to these key principles, there are several areas where PRINCE2 Agile leverages the strengths of both approaches to provide a *more effective* environment than either approach can deliver independently, specifically in:

- Business value generation
- Management of project variables
- Communication and reporting.

Each of these is explained in more detail below.

Business value generation

The relentless pursuit of high business-value outcomes is one of the strongest parallels between PRINCE2 and Agile methods, whether these are quantitative benefits (e.g. increased profits, reduced overhead costs) or qualitative benefits (e.g. more satisfied customers, greater employee retention).[25]

In PRINCE2, each project must provide sufficient business-value justification in the project brief for the initial project funding and resources to be approved. The PID then needs to expand upon this by providing an achievable approach for delivering this business value. Without these two documents (and other supporting PRINCE2 artifacts), the Project Board cannot – and will not – grant approval for the project to proceed.

As the project progresses, the Project Board requires confirmation of ongoing business-value delivery *at each*

---

[25] AXELOS provides Management of Value (MoV) guidelines to distinguish between the perceived and actual benefits a solution provides for the organization. Section 9.4, *PRINCE2 Agile*, Keith Richards, AXELOS (2015), *www.axelos.com/store/book/prince2-agile*.

Chapter 3: Overview of PRINCE2 Agile

project stage (in accordance with the benefits review plan) before granting approval for the next project stage to progress.

At the closure of the project, the business value that the project generated is formally documented as one of the key metrics of project success.

In Agile methods, business-value generation is the primary driver in determining which capabilities are at the top of the product backlog for the project delivery team to work on as their next priority. The main difference is that, for Agile methods, the product owner is generally the role that is responsible for deciding what capabilities will deliver the greatest business value as part of the planning for each delivery cycle – and then confirming whether the expected business value was achieved at each review session. In Agile methods, the level of involvement of more senior management in the decision-making process is generally left to the discretion of the product owner.

In PRINCE2 Agile, both of these approaches are combined, as shown in the "Requirements as Outcomes," "Acceptance criteria," and "Outputs" touchpoints in *Figure 5*. The business value that was originally identified in the PRINCE2 Agile project brief (and elaborated upon in the PRINCE2 Agile PID) creates the foundation for the project product definition, which feeds directly into the priority-driven product backlog that the project delivery team uses in their Agile work.

The key difference is that, in PRINCE2 Agile, there are *several people* involved in defining and confirming the delivered outputs:

- The executive, who is responsible for confirming the business case and ensuring that the project delivers its intended business value.
- The senior user(s), who have the ultimate decision-making authority on the capabilities of the solution, including identifying the *minimum viable product* (MVP).

Chapter 3: Overview of PRINCE2 Agile

- The product owner(s) and customer subject matter experts (CSMEs),[26] who
  - identify the detailed requirements, the corresponding acceptance criteria and the priorities for the project delivery team.
  - work hands-on with the project delivery team to identify the highest-priority work for each iteration/release.
  - review the outputs from each iteration/release and confirm whether they meet the acceptance criteria.
- The business ambassador(s),[27] who are optional staff to further support the project delivery team by providing subject-matter expertise as input, but not by making the final decision on priorities (as this is done by the product owners).
- The business analysts and requirements engineers, who are optional staff able to provide additional support to the project delivery team in researching, eliciting and communicating requirements, as well as creating required documentation.

This is a significant shift from Agile methods, where the product owner is often the single source of business requirements identification, prioritization, and confirmation, even for complex solutions across multiple business areas. In PRINCE2 Agile, there is significantly more involvement across the organization, including confirmation and support from executive management.

---

[26] On larger projects – or ones that cover a broad spectrum of capabilities – there may be a need to have multiple people serve as product owners and CSMEs.

[27] In DSDM, the business ambassador is a representative from the business area who provides input (clarification) to the project delivery team on requirements from the business perspective.

Chapter 3: Overview of PRINCE2 Agile

Management of project variables

Traditional project management approaches tend to focus on the management of Cost, Time and Scope as the three most important variables to control on a project.[28] When there is a change in these variables (for example, the customer wants the product delivered three weeks ahead of schedule), these traditional approaches also guide project managers on how to adjust the other two variables to keep the project on track. In this example, where Time is reduced, the project manager can negotiate for a corresponding reduction in the Scope of the work delivered and/or an increase in the Cost of delivery to supplement the available resources.

The original Project Management Triangle has been expanded over time to include Quality as a fourth variable, where a reduction in Time or Cost – or an increase in Scope – can be compensated for by reducing the amount of effort expended by the project team on testing the output or confirming its usability. (There are multiple reasons why sacrificing Quality is never the correct option, but that alone would completely fill another book!)

In PRINCE2 Agile, the management of project tolerances is expanded upon even further to include the management of:

- Benefits
- Scope
- Time
- Cost
- Quality
- Risk.

---

[28] This is also known as the "Project Management Triangle": *https://programsuccess.wordpress.com/2011/05/02/scope-time-and-cost-managing-the-triple-constraint*.

Chapter 3: Overview of PRINCE2 Agile

For each of these management tolerances, the Project Board determines what are the baseline acceptable levels for project success, and to what extent the project is permitted to vary from these tolerances before an exception needs to be raised for Project Board review.

The interesting thing is that, unlike traditional projects that would monitor all of these tolerances with equal scrutiny, PRINCE2 Agile projects take a different perspective, seeing:

- Time and Cost as *fixed values* that are not expected to vary as the project progresses (i.e. "Don't Flex").
- Scope and Quality as *flexible values* that are likely to vary as the project progresses (i.e. "Flex").
- Benefits and Risk as *possibly flexible values* that could, at the discretion of the Project Board and the project manager, be adjusted as the project progresses (i.e. "Might Flex").

The reasoning behind each of these is explained in the following sections.

Time and budget management as *fixed values*

In PRINCE2, the management of project timelines and budgets is generally achieved by identifying fixed values up front and establishing tolerances for reporting exceptions if the project work is substantially over or under these allocations.

In PRINCE2 Agile, it is expected that work will be undertaken by a *known team* (with an *established overhead cost*) and will be delivered in *agreed timeframes* (generally time-boxed intervals). This is why, in PRINCE2 Agile, the originally established project timelines and budgets *are not expected to vary* throughout the project delivery.

PRINCE2 Agile focuses more on managing the *value* of the *outputs* that the project delivery team produces within these fixed times and costs. This includes getting updates on which high-value capabilities the team has delivered in each agreed timeframe, how much business value these capabilities are generating, and how

Chapter 3: Overview of PRINCE2 Agile

well these capabilities meet business expectations.[29]

Scope and Quality as *flexible values*

On the other end of the spectrum are the two management variables in a PRINCE2 Agile project which are, by their very nature, intended to be flexible: Scope and Quality.

The "Business-value generation" section above described how the business requirements that are identified in the PRINCE2 Agile project brief (and elaborated upon in the PRINCE2 Agile PID) create the foundation for the product definition which feeds directly into the priority-driven product backlog that the project delivery team uses in their Agile work. Key to this is the *priority-driven* product backlog.

Agile methods understand that not every capability requested by the business is of an equal priority – and that there is greater value in focusing the project delivery team on producing the highest-priority capabilities. Although the product owner is encouraged to document the full scope of requirements for the solution (including any known high-, medium-, and low-priority capabilities), they are also expected to put these requirements in order of top-down priority, to keep the most valuable capabilities as the primary focus of the project delivery team in the limited time they have for each upcoming iteration/release.

---

[29] There is one caveat to consider in fixing the Cost variable on a PRINCE2 Agile project. The focus of this section has been on the fixed cost of the project delivery team, i.e. the human-resources cost for the project. As each project progresses, there is the possibility of other unexpected costs arising, for example unexpected software license fees or additional hardware that needs to be purchased. In these situations, the Project Board may want the project manager to keep team costs as a fixed value, but may establish tolerances for other project expenses.

Chapter 3: Overview of PRINCE2 Agile

As PRINCE2 Agile projects have fixed budgets and fixed timeframes (and, therefore, a limited number of iterations/releases where the project delivery team can produce outputs), it is expected that not every capability that is listed on the product backlog will be delivered by the team. In fact, one of the primary purposes of PRINCE2 Agile is to ensure that projects are continued (or stopped) on the basis of how much ongoing business value they are able to deliver to the organization. When a project has reached a point where the only work remaining is the delivery of the low business-value capabilities that remain on the backlog, the Project Board can – and should – consider closing the project and investing the available resources in activities that will generate more business value across the organization.

It is also expected that the priorities that were originally established at the start of the project will need to be adjusted over time to reflect the information that is obtained from ongoing development work, as well as changes that may occur in the organization and the market.

For all of these reasons, it is important in PRINCE2 Agile that the Scope of the project work be flexible to support these expected variations. Where possible, the business case should be: "defined in a flexible way to allow for what is being delivered (and its value) to change to a degree during the project."[30] This allows minor changes to be accommodated in the project delivery using the selected Agile method, and only involves raising an exception to the Project Board where there are major changes that could affect the core business outcomes, require changes to the project business case, or stop the project altogether.

---

[30] Section 4.1.3.4, *PRINCE2 Agile*, Keith Richards, AXELOS (2015), www.axelos.com/store/book/prince2-agile.

Chapter 3: Overview of PRINCE2 Agile

Similarly, the acceptance criteria (i.e. the quality criteria) that are established for the expected capabilities of the solution are intended to be a combination of those that are *essential* (i.e. the product cannot be released unless it meets these minimum standards) and those that are *desirable* (i.e. there is a preference for the product to meet the qualification, but the approval for product release will not be withheld if it does not). Although the project delivery team will endeavor to meet as many of the acceptance criteria (i.e. quality criteria) as possible within the allocated timeframe, their primary focus will be on achieving the essential criteria to ensure that they are producing potentially releasable outputs. Therefore the Quality of the project work needs to be flexible to allow for the possibility of some (or all) of the desirable acceptance criteria not being achieved, especially where the cost of meeting desirable criteria does not justify the amount of value that the organization will receive from this additional work.

In PRINCE2 Agile, the senior user(s) and the product owner identify the quality metrics (and tolerances) for measuring the success and acceptance of the delivered outputs (i.e. the definition of "done"). These metrics are described at a high level in the project product description; defined at a more detailed level in each of the epics, user stories, and technical stories in the product backlog; and used as the basis for ongoing testing to determine when each of the required capabilities has achieved the intended outcome.

Benefits and Risk as *possibly flexible values*

In PRINCE2 Agile, the level of flexibility that is acceptable for the Benefits that a project will deliver – and the amount of Risk that the Project Board will tolerate – both need to be determined on a case-by-case basis for each project.

For some PRINCE2 Agile projects, there will be strict senior management expectations of the Benefits that the project will deliver for the organization (and, therefore, a *minimum viable business case* that must be achieved to justify the investment in the project team) – for example, a product that is intended to

Chapter 3: Overview of PRINCE2 Agile

meet a legislative requirement by a specific date. In these situations, the Project Board may have no flexibility in varying the stated benefits in the PID.

For other projects, there could be a significant amount of flexibility, particularly where the Benefits identified in the project brief are described at a high level (or with a range of options) and it is left to the discretion of the Project Board to determine whether they have been achieved. For example, a new issue logging system that is intended to provide better customer service may have a stated benefit of reducing the volume and frequency of support calls, but, until the system is released and its impact measured, the ability for it to achieve the intended benefit may need to be a preemptive judgment call by the Project Board.

Similarly, the amount of Risk that the Project Board is willing to accept could vary based on the nature of the project or the organizational culture. For a particularly risk-averse Project Board – or a particularly high-profile project – there may be no flexibility in the acceptable level of Risk, i.e. zero tolerance. This means that *every* potential risk to the project needs to be reported as an exception and reviewed.

Equally, there are projects where a reasonable amount of Risk is considered tolerable by the Project Board as long as it does not represent a significant risk to the core business outcomes. In these situations, the Project Board may be comfortable establishing risk tolerances for the project manager to report on only when they have been exceeded.

As PRINCE2 Agile can be applied to a wide variety of projects, it is impractical for there to be a fixed definition of acceptable Benefits or acceptable Risk for any one project. The level of flexibility that is appropriate for each project needs to be left to the discretion of the Project Board.

Communication and reporting

In PRINCE2 Agile, there is an unprecedented level of ongoing communication between the Project Board and the project

Chapter 3: Overview of PRINCE2 Agile

delivery team with communication tools that provide all stakeholders with regular updates on project status, issues, and risks. This communication is generally available through *information radiators* that are maintained by the project delivery team and are visible in their work area (where stakeholders are colocated) or through electronic delivery channels (where stakeholders are remote).

To ensure the effective governance and management of project objectives, PRINCE2 Agile provides the Project Board with the same level of information on project status, issues, risks, and adherence to defined tolerances as PRINCE2, including highlight reports, checkpoint reports, stage reports, issue registers, risk registers, configuration item records, and exception reports. With PRINCE2 Agile, however, the communication tools described can *supplement* the standard reporting tools in PRINCE2 with the most current project information available. In some situations, these communication tools can also serve as a *replacement* for PRINCE2 reports and registers that the project manager had previously needed to maintain manually.

Where project issues and risks have been identified (through either the Agile communication tools, the PRINCE2 reporting tools, or a combination), these are addressed with the same level of scrutiny and follow-through in PRINCE2 Agile, although the mechanisms for achieving this may be different depending on how the project is structured.

For teams using Scrum, one approach is to have the project delivery team raise issues in the daily stand-up session (for the team manager/Scrummaster to record), to empower the team to try to resolve the issues and risks within the iteration, and, if they cannot be resolved in that timeframe, to escalate them to the project manager. Another approach is to have the project delivery team record all issues and risks in a centralized location (manual or electronic) throughout the iteration, give the team manager/Scrummaster the responsibility of initially vetting these, and then escalating the most critical ones – or those that cannot be immediately resolved by the project delivery team – for resolution by the project manager.

Whatever approach is utilized by the project team, the most important requirement is that there are appropriate channels for anyone on the project team to raise issues and identify risks, that they are recorded in an accessible location, and that there is an agreed procedure for escalating issues and risks that require input from the Project Board.

Further detail on how to select the most appropriate communication and reporting tools for your project is provided in the implementation guidelines that begin in *Chapter 5: Moving from PRINCE2 to PRINCE2 Agile*.

More information on PRINCE2 Agile is provided in the *Bibliography*.

CHAPTER 4: FIVE KEYS TO PRINCE2 AGILE SUCCESS

Implementing PRINCE2 Agile is more than understanding the principles and processes that drive the framework. For PRINCE2 Agile to deliver high business-value outcomes, you need to ensure that you have an organization, a project, and a team that are positioned to maximize its effectiveness – and that you establish the most suitable approach for your environment.

The following are five key factors that can influence the success of your PRINCE2 Agile projects, and recommendations for addressing the challenges that might occur for each. In reviewing these factors, it is important to note that the decision to implement PRINCE2 Agile is often a question of determining what the ideal approach is for your environment (that is, by asking the questions "How Agile can we be?" and "What do we need to change in order to be more Agile?"). It is rarely a "yes/no" question whether or not to use PRINCE2 Agile altogether.

To address these questions, the official PRINCE2 Agile guide provides readers with an Agilometer,[31] a six-point sliding scale that can assist organizations in determining the extent to which Agile methods can be used for their projects. The Agilometer can be used both for the initial assessment before the project begins, and as a comparison baseline to assess the effectiveness of ongoing project work, and to apply adjustments as needed.

It is recommended that you use the Agilometer as part of your evaluation of the following five key factors in determining the

---

[31] Chapter 24, *PRINCE2 Agile*, Keith Richards, AXELOS (2015), *www.axelos.com/store/book/prince2-agile*.

The first key to PRINCE2 Agile success: *the right organization*

PRINCE2 Agile is more than a framework; it is a *mindset*. For PRINCE2 Agile projects to be successful, you need an environment of trust, teamwork, open communication, flexibility, continuous improvement, and allowing people to fulfill their potential.

You may also need executive management to be open to committing funds based on a more broadly defined business case, i.e. without having a detailed upfront specification or without a commitment to exact functionality being delivered on a specific date.

If your organization is forward-thinking enough to provide staff with the trust and empowerment that PRINCE2 Agile requires – and to appreciate the benefits that this responsive approach can deliver in an ever-changing, fast-moving marketplace – then your project is better positioned to successfully deliver outcomes using this framework.

If, however, your organization is more focused on heavy management (i.e. distrustful of staff), prefers to issue top-down directives without staff consultation, or discourages open communication within and across departments, then leveraging the benefits of PRINCE2 Agile may be more of a challenge for you. That is not to say that the PRINCE2 Agile framework cannot be implemented in these environments; it is a caveat that there are likely to be more significant overheads (i.e. more formal and frequent status reporting, less flexibility to adapt functionality based on emergent information, more time required for Project Board members to negotiate ongoing work). Each additional overhead reduces the efficiencies and benefits that PRINCE2 Agile can deliver for the organization.

The closer you can get to working in an empowering, trusting, open-communication environment – even if the Project Board

Chapter 4: Five Keys to PRINCE2 Agile Success

members need to create this environment as a *microcosm* within the organization – the more likely it is that you will deliver a successful PRINCE2 Agile project.

The second key to PRINCE2 Agile success: *the right motivation*

In addition to having (or creating) the right working environment for PRINCE2 Agile to thrive, it is important for you to recognize *why* PRINCE2 Agile is being implemented for this project in the first place. Is executive management interested in adding more flexible governance in order to increase team productivity or the relevance and quality of deliverables? Does the project delivery team want a greater awareness of the business drivers for the work that they are doing? Or is implementing PRINCE2 Agile a compliance mandate (or a customer request) that the team is *required* to fulfill without having a strong interest in – or a genuine appreciation of – the framework?

Understanding the motivation for the move to PRINCE2 Agile will help you to determine the degree to which the framework is incorporated, the most appropriate approach to select within the framework, and the areas where additional team education may be required for PRINCE2 Agile to be successful.

If you find that the motivation for implementing PRINCE2 Agile is from the organization or from external stakeholders – and not from the people on the project team – then it is likely that PRINCE2 Agile will be implemented in practice, but not in spirit. Similarly, if the motivation is coming exclusively from the Project Board without input from the project delivery team – or the opposite – you may find that the necessary project roles will be assigned and the correct documentation will be created (i.e. it will *look like* a PRINCE2 Agile project on paper), but the team may not fully appreciate, or adhere to, the core underlying principles that distinguish PRINCE2 Agile from waterfall projects or from ungoverned Agile projects.

Chapter 4: Five Keys to PRINCE2 Agile Success

The previous section identified the challenges that your project might face when the overall organizational culture is not ideal for the PRINCE2 Agile framework. In some cases, not having a supporting organizational culture can become an insurmountable challenge that makes PRINCE2 Agile difficult (if not impossible) to implement effectively.

If the issue is that the motivation for implementing PRINCE2 Agile is not coming from the project team, addressing this challenge can be as simple as supplementing the team's formal PRINCE2 Agile education with collaborative sessions that focus on the spirit of the framework and the benefits for the project.

For current PRINCE2 practitioners, this education may need to focus on the value in empowering the team, encouraging open communication, and having flexible product descriptions that can be adapted as the project progresses. For current Agile practitioners, this education can equally focus on the value of having greater management support, more awareness of business drivers, and status reporting with fewer overheads.

Even if the original motivation for implementing PRINCE2 Agile did not come from the entire project team, you have an opportunity to address this early in the project and ensure that the implementation of PRINCE2 Agile is more than having the team meticulously following a framework without maximizing the benefits that it can deliver.

The third key to PRINCE2 Agile success: *the right project*

PRINCE2 Agile can be a highly effective framework when it is used for projects that are well suited to Agile delivery, specifically:

- Projects where business stakeholders are available to work with the project delivery team throughout the project lifecycle.
- Projects where the technology platform supports incremental delivery.

Chapter 4: Five Keys to PRINCE2 Agile Success

- Projects with development teams that have four to eight people (or larger development teams that can be distributed into integrated smaller teams using methods like Scrum or Scrums or the Scaled Agile Framework).

If your project meets all of the above criteria, it is likely to be well suited to Agile delivery, and you can progress to the "*right people*" section below.

If your project does not meet one or more of the criteria, you may be able to apply selected Agile practices in your project work (e.g. daily stand-up meetings, information radiators), but it is likely that you will not be able to leverage the full benefits of the PRINCE2 Agile framework.

For example, if the technology platform that you are using does not support incremental delivery of functionality (e.g. fixed enterprise platforms, mainframes, legacy systems), you may be able to have the team work on the highest-priority capabilities using time-boxed intervals, but the benefits of leveraging what they are building in a live environment may be restricted to the end of the project (or may not occur at all if the project ends earlier than expected).

This does not restrict the project team from going forward with a PRINCE2 Agile framework, but it does impact how PRINCE2 Agile is implemented and it may affect the benefits that can be achieved. It is critical information to include in the Agilometer and in your assessment of the extent to which Agile methods can be used for your project.[32]

---

[32] It may also be valuable for you to consider using the Cynefin framework to determine the level of uncertainty in your project. See Section 17.4.1, *PRINCE2 Agile*, Keith Richards, AXELOS (2015), *www.axelos.com/store/book/prince2-agile*.

Chapter 4: Five Keys to PRINCE2 Agile Success

The fourth key to PRINCE2 Agile success: *the right people*

As described above, PRINCE2 Agile is as much a *mindset* and an *attitude* as it is a framework. For PRINCE2 Agile to be successful, all of the project team members need to be prepared to work in an environment of trust, empowerment, teamwork, open communication, flexibility, and continuous improvement.

For the Project Board members and the project manager, this could mean trading off the direct control of project activities that they have had in the past in favor of entrusting the project delivery team members to take ownership of their work and to be responsible for communicating significant information as the project progresses.

For project delivery team members, this could mean taking greater ownership and responsibility for delivering agreed outcomes, as well as *actively* communicating project status information (instead of waiting for the project manager to ask them for a status report).

This type of open and trusting environment can be a welcome change to the "command-and-control" projects that people have worked on in the past. It can, however, also be extremely uncomfortable for some people to relinquish their control, to take more responsibility for their work, to become more communicative, or to focus on team success over personal gains.

Where you have the discretion to select project team members who are ideally suited to the PRINCE2 Agile environment, it is beneficial to look for people who are strong communicators, who are willing to take responsibility for their work, who can trust other team members to deliver on their commitments, and who strive to continuously review and refine the process to ensure that the team is positioned to deliver excellence throughout the project. People who have previous experience working on PRINCE2 Agile projects (or on well-executed Agile projects) are more likely to flourish in this environment – and to encourage others on the team to do the same.

Chapter 4: Five Keys to PRINCE2 Agile Success

Where there is limited opportunity to choose other staff for this work – and some (or all) of the project team members are uncomfortable in this type of working environment – you may need to decide whether these challenges can be addressed with the proper guidance, e.g. training and mentoring. It may be that the team members have reservations because they have never worked in that type of environment before and, with some exposure, they will begin to see the value and embrace the approach. It may also be that they are going outside their comfort zone and need the support of an experienced PRINCE2 Agile (or Agile) practitioner to pair with them and give them confidence.

As with the other factors, having people who are uncomfortable with (or resistant to) the PRINCE2 Agile environment is not necessarily a deal breaker, but it is important to include this in your assessment of the extent to which Agile methods can be used.

The fifth key to PRINCE2 Agile success: *the right approach*

Implementing PRINCE2 Agile is not an exact science with strict instructions that apply equally to every project and every organizational culture – it is a *framework* with guidelines that you can adjust and adapt to the specific needs of each project.

In those circumstances where the Project Board, the project manager and the project delivery team are located in the same offices with a culture of openness and high communication, ongoing status reporting may be achieved by having an information radiator prominently displayed outside the delivery team's work area – supplemented by highlight reports, checkpoint reports, end stage reports, and exception reports, where required.

In circumstances where the Project Board and the project delivery team are in physically separate locations (or the delivery team itself is spread across multiple locations), the traditional wall displays may need to be supplemented by electronic status reporting tools such as online burndown charts

Chapter 4: Five Keys to PRINCE2 Agile Success

or issue registers. Equally, if the Project Board and the project delivery team do not have a long history of working together – and the organization is new to Agile methods – the project manager may need to create supplemental status updates and other lines of communication to keep the Project Board appraised of the project status and confident about continuing to use PRINCE2 Agile.

The following chapters provide step-by-step advice on how to implement PRINCE2 Agile, specific to the needs of your project and your organization. They focus on the five most likely situations that an organization will encounter in the implementation of PRINCE2 Agile:

- moving from PRINCE2 to PRINCE2 Agile
- merging existing PRINCE2 and Agile methods
- moving an existing waterfall project to PRINCE2 Agile
- implementing a new PRINCE2 Agile project with no existing framework
- implementing a new PRINCE2 Agile project with an existing Agile delivery team.

In each chapter, recommendations and alternatives are provided specific to each project situation, allowing you to choose the approach that is most suited to your organizational culture, your project requirements, and your project team.

It may be helpful for you to refer back to *Figure 1* to determine which chapter(s) are the most relevant to your specific needs.

CHAPTER 5: MOVING FROM PRINCE2 TO PRINCE2 AGILE

Expanding an existing PRINCE2 framework to the PRINCE2 Agile framework is likely to be the most common project scenario that readers will be facing. This chapter provides you with step-by-step advice on setting up and executing your PRINCE2 Agile project when your organization is in a position to leverage your existing PRINCE2 framework.

Which came first?

There is always a "chicken-and-egg" trade-off in project planning. Although the steps in this chapter are listed in sequential order, Steps 1 to 7 can (and should) be implemented *in parallel* based on emerging project information. For example, identifying the project team in Step 1 may need to be revisited after the release plan is defined in Step 4 to align proposed timelines with staff availability. In this case, part of the project team can be identified up front and other team members will need to be added as the project planning progresses (and, ideally, given the opportunity to provide ongoing input into the project planning).

Similarly, the project team's ability to define the project controls and tolerances in Step 6 may depend upon the tools that are selected in Step 5, e.g. where the Project Board is comfortable increasing some of the tolerances because the communication tools selected in Step 5 give them greater ongoing access to current information on project status.

The objective is to use the information gathered in Steps 1 to 6 to build the PID in Step 7, either as

- a progressive activity (where project information is added to the PID as each key decision is made in Steps 1 to 6), or as

Chapter 5: Moving From PRINCE2 to PRINCE2 Agile

- a cumulative activity (where all of the project information is added to the PID once Steps 1 to 6 are completed to minimize the potential for rework if key decisions need to be adjusted in the ongoing project planning).

As you complete each step, it may be valuable to stop and revisit the decisions that were made in the previous steps to confirm whether they are still valid or need to be adjusted based on the subsequent decisions made by the team.

Step 1: Identify the right project team

Implementing a successful PRINCE2 Agile project requires a *collaborative effort* between the Project Board members, the project manager, and the project delivery team members. This includes key decisions that need to be made *at the start of the project* to establish the most effective team structure, delivery approach, communication tools, quality management strategy, risk management strategy, configuration management strategy, and methods for implementing project controls. It also includes the ongoing review and adjustment of the selected approaches to ensure their continued effectiveness.

Involving all members of the project team in these initial decisions creates an environment of high communication, transparency, empowerment, and ownership that carries forward throughout the project delivery, leveraging one of the most powerful advantages of the PRINCE2 Agile framework.

It is, therefore, important to identify the core Project Board, the project manager, and the project delivery team members *as early as possible* in the process to confirm their availability and to enlist their participation in these initial planning decisions.

For some projects, the Project Board members and project manager may have already been identified (or their roles in the organization may make them the definitive choices). Where these team members have already been decided, it is important to ensure that they are familiar with the structure and principles of the PRINCE2 Agile framework – and the distinction from their previous PRINCE2 work – before the project begins, and to assess their comfort level with this approach. For example,

Chapter 5: Moving From PRINCE2 to PRINCE2 Agile

Project Board members who are looking for a "command-and-control" project governance structure may not be well suited to a PRINCE2 Agile delivery model (or may require the establishment of additional project controls to address their concerns).

Where there is discretion in choosing the Project Board members and the project manager, the preference would be to choose people who have the characteristics that make an effective PRINCE2 Agile project team member. (See "The fourth key to PRINCE2 Agile success: *the right people*" in *Chapter 4: Five Keys to PRINCE2 Agile Success* for further detail.)

Similarly, for the project delivery team, there may already be an established delivery team (or the skills that are required for project delivery may determine which people are selected). If there is discretion in choosing the project delivery team members, use the same approach described for selecting the Project Board members and project manager, with a preference for people who are familiar and comfortable with the PRINCE2 Agile framework – and, ideally, experienced in the Agile method that will be used for project delivery.[33]

Once you have identified the core project team members, the next step is to identify the most effective team structure and roles – and to decide if there are additional people that need to be added to the project team. This includes:

- Determining if there are people needed on the Project Board in addition to the executive, senior user(s) and senior supplier(s) – and what their respective responsibilities will be.

---

[33] This may not be possible until the appropriate Agile method for that project is selected, in which case the selection of resources may need to be revisited.

Chapter 5: Moving From PRINCE2 to PRINCE2 Agile

- Determining who is needed to accurately represent the full requirements for the project deliverables in addition to the senior user, including customer subject matter expert(s), product owner(s), business ambassador(s), business analyst(s), and requirements engineers(s) – identifying their respective responsibilities and how they will interact with each other to confirm accuracy and consistency.
- Determining whether the project requires a separately assigned team manager or whether the project manager (or, for Scrum projects, the Scrummaster) will effectively function in this role.
- Determining the respective roles on the project delivery team, based on the Agile method selected (if it is known at this point in the process).

The outcome from these decisions may require the team to review and adjust the staff that were originally identified for the core project team, and to include these additional people in the ongoing planning discussions, where possible.

Step 2: Establish a shared vision

Once the project team is identified, it is important to ensure that everyone on the team has a shared vision of what the project is intended to deliver and how the PRINCE2 Agile principles and practices will be implemented to achieve these objectives.

If this is the first project that this team is delivering with PRINCE2 Agile (even if they have worked on PRINCE2 projects before), it is strongly recommended that all project participants – including the members of the Project Board, the project manager, and the project delivery team – get together for an interactive workshop to establish a shared understanding of PRINCE2 Agile and to set the focus for ongoing work. This can be done either as a separate session or as the first part of the project planning session(s).

Chapter 5: Moving From PRINCE2 to PRINCE2 Agile

Once the team has a common understanding of PRINCE2 Agile, the workshop session(s) should focus on establishing a shared vision of the key project information, including:

- The product vision and product roadmap.
- The expected benefits that the product will deliver.
- The overall project timeline, including the intended stages and releases, and any fixed dates that the project must adhere to, e.g. launch dates for marketing campaigns (with emphasis on the Agile method for delivering the highest-priority business capabilities within these timeframes).
- Any known issues and risks.
- The identified project roles.
- The preferred Agile method for product delivery, e.g. Scrum, Lean, Kanban, Scrumban (with a revisit of the project roles and team members as needed based on this decision).
- The team's preferred methods for communication, status reporting, issue management, risk management, and configuration management.
- Other team and organizational culture dynamics, such as the extent to which the project delivery team will be empowered to make decisions and self-organize.

In this session, the project team will also need to determine how the work packages being delivered by the team will be managed and communicated with the project manager. There are several potential options, including:

- Assigning a dedicated team manager to manage the work packages and update the project manager on the progress of the team's work.
- Having the project manager serve as the team manager to manage the work packages.
- If the team is using Scrum or Scrumban as their Agile method, having the Scrummaster serve as the team manager.

Chapter 5: Moving From PRINCE2 to PRINCE2 Agile

The session may also include the team establishing a shared understanding of the terminology that will be used and, if needed, creating a glossary of these terms.

The outcomes from the workshop session(s) will set the stage for the decisions that need to be made in the following steps and documented in the PID. Equally important, it will engage the entire project team and create a shared ownership of the project and the outcomes.

Step 3: Define the outcomes and outputs

The PRINCE2 Agile framework makes a distinction between the *outcomes* of a project, i.e. the measurable business value that the project generates,[34] and the *outputs* of a project, i.e. the specific project deliverables that are produced by the team to achieve these outcomes.

The intended project outcomes and benefits will have been described as a high-level business case in the project brief that was used for the initial project approval. As part of the project planning, these high-level requirements will need to be defined as more detailed business outcomes with the associated benefits and acceptance criteria identified.

The senior user generally provides this additional information, including identifying what is considered an MVP for release, distinguishing between the mandatory and the "nice-to-have" features and, where appropriate, identifying the range of tolerances in the acceptance criteria.[35] These product capabilities are documented in the product description (which may already exist at a program level) and in the project product

---

[34] For further information, see Gabrielle Benefield's guide to creating measurable outcomes at *www.gabriellebenefield.com/mobius/how-to-measure-value*.

[35] With the executive having the ultimate responsibility for ensuring that the intended benefits are being achieved.

Chapter 5: Moving From PRINCE2 to PRINCE2 Agile

description (which are the subset of product capabilities that this specific project is intended to deliver), with corresponding benefits identified in the benefits review plan.[36]

Once the detailed business outcomes are identified, the next step is for the product owner(s) to transform these requirements into outputs (i.e. discrete bodies of work) that can be estimated and produced by the project delivery team. Additional support for this may be provided by the CSMEs, business ambassadors and other product specialists where needed (with the potential for further help from business analysts and requirements engineers).

In Agile methods, these outputs would generally be

- Defined as epics, user stories, and technical stories (for nonfunctional requirements) with acceptance criteria identified for each.
- Put into top-down priority order in a product backlog (and, if required, a release backlog).
- Reviewed in interactive sessions with the project delivery team in accordance with the selected Agile method (e.g. sprint planning sessions).
- Populated into the appropriate Agile tools for product delivery, e.g. sprint backlog, Kanban board.

Where possible, the PID should maintain *high-level descriptions* of product capabilities, referring out to the detail provided in these Agile tools for more specific information. Similarly, the benefits review plan should ideally focus on the outcomes, not the outputs. This allows for the outputs to be adjusted as the project progresses without compromising the agreed outcomes.

---

[36] To support the adaptability and responsiveness of Agile methods, it is preferred that any capabilities identified by the senior user are described with flexibility to allow for the outputs to be adjusted as the project progresses without compromising the agreed outcomes.

Chapter 5: Moving From PRINCE2 to PRINCE2 Agile

Step 4: Define the release plan

In **Step 2: Establish a shared vision**, it was identified that one of the key project areas for the team to discuss is the overall project timeline, including the intended stages and releases, and any fixed dates that the project must adhere to. In waterfall methods, the stages, releases and fixed dates that are identified at the beginning of a project are generally tied to specific capabilities (i.e. outputs) that are expected to be delivered within each timeframe. Establishing these upfront expectations for specific capabilities at specific times creates one of the biggest challenges (and, one could argue, weaknesses) of waterfall methods, as it minimizes the flexibility that the project team needs to adapt the outputs to support emergent information as the project progresses. It can also create significant overheads (and potential delays) for the project team where changes to outputs need to be treated as exceptions and formally approved before the project delivery team can progress.

PRINCE2 Agile provides a balanced view between giving executive management the timeframes that are needed for forward planning, and giving project teams the flexibility that is needed to continue progressing their work. This is primarily achieved by establishing stages and release dates that are tied to high level business outcomes – not specific functionality – and by allowing the PRINCE2 Agile process to guide the project work to achieve these outcomes.

PRINCE2 Agile also addresses the need for project adaptability by allowing the work that is undertaken to proceed using an Agile model, where time is generally managed as a fixed value with the variability being *what is delivered* in that timeframe.

For example, a project that is allocated for a duration of six months may be broken down into six time-boxed iterations of one month each. Within each iteration, the project delivery team strives to deliver as many of the highest-priority capabilities that the team can produce. At the end of the six months, the project delivery team will have delivered a cumulative set of highest-priority capabilities which, ideally,

Chapter 5: Moving From PRINCE2 to PRINCE2 Agile

corresponds to the stages and the release plan that were identified at the start of the project (and updated as the project progressed).

This is an important distinction when it comes to distinguishing PRINCE2 Agile from other governance methods. Establishing stages, release plans, and other fixed dates at the start of a project should be viewed as an *initial starting point* (a baseline) that is likely to be adjusted as the project progresses.

The more the capabilities that will be delivered in these timelines can be defined at a high level, i.e. specific to outcomes, not outputs, the greater flexibility the project delivery team has to deliver the highest-priority business capabilities that will achieve these business outcomes within these timeframes (including allowing these capabilities to be released into live environments for ongoing measurement).

To achieve the PRINCE2 Agile planning model, the project team should group the intended capabilities of the solution into an initial time-boxed plan for intended stages and releases with the understanding that this is a *baseline for moving the project forward* and that the outcomes of ongoing project work will be used to confirm or adjust the release plan.

It is left to the discretion of each project team to determine the relationship between stages, releases, and iterations, e.g. to determine whether:

- there can be multiple releases within a stage
- releases should only occur once at the end of each stage
- capabilities can be released into the live environment as soon as they have successfully passed acceptance testing, without waiting for a defined project timeframe.[37]

---

[37] Figures 16.2, 16.3, and 16.4 in the AXELOS official PRINCE2 Agile guide provide further detail on the options and alternatives available for planning iterations, releases, and stages.

Chapter 5: Moving From PRINCE2 to PRINCE2 Agile

Once the high-level project plan is identified, the planning of the work for each iteration/release is undertaken by the project delivery team using the selected Agile method and guided by the top-down priorities identified by the product owner. At the end of the agreed time, the project delivery team will review the work that was produced with the product owner and work jointly to determine what should be included in the next iteration/release.

Depending on the level of uncertainty of the intended capabilities, the project team may also want to include a dedicated time-boxed interval for upfront investigation, experimentation, and prototyping to address potential risks. This allocated upfront time is commonly referred to as the Discovery Phase (e.g. Sprint Zero in the Scrum method). This phase can also be used for other work required to initiate the project, including purchasing equipment and configuring technology platforms.

As the project progresses, if there are substantial changes to the originally agreed release plan, the project manager is responsible for informing the Project Board of the exception for their guidance and approval to proceed.

Step 5: Choose your tools

As identified in *Chapter 4: Five Keys to PRINCE2 Agile Success*, one of the most critical factors in implementing PRINCE2 Agile successfully is establishing an environment of *transparency*, *collaboration*, and *communication*. This is particularly important for:

- communication within the project delivery team (including remote team members)
- communication between the project delivery team and the project manager and
- communication between the project delivery team and the Project Board (where the project manager may or may not need to be an intermediary, as described in the following section).

Chapter 5: Moving From PRINCE2 to PRINCE2 Agile

The Project Board needs to trust and empower the project delivery team to produce the required outputs, but they also need the opportunity to see the team's progress and to receive advanced knowledge of potential issues and risks throughout the project timeline, if they choose. Equally, the project delivery team wants the ability to keep the project manager and Project Board informed without required substantial additional overheads or needing to shift focus from their primary work. There are several tools available in the PRINCE2 Agile framework that can address both of these requirements *without requiring significant additional work* from the project delivery team, including:

- ***Information radiators*** that are prominently displayed in work areas (or online) to show vision statements, daily progress, burndowns, planned work, and potential issues.
- ***Executive dashboards*** that provide a summary of key project information as "at-a-glance" management reports (and, with the right Agile tools, can be *automatically* updated when the team updates the backlogs).
- ***Iteration review sessions*** that provide the product owner and the project manager (and optionally the Project Board) with demonstrations of the capabilities produced in each iteration.
- ***Daily stand-up meetings*** which include a review of potential hurdles (i.e. issues) that can be recorded by team managers (or project managers if they are attending).

It is also possible for the team to create online tools for logging issues, risks, and configuration items in shared locations which are easily accessible by all project team members.

PRINCE2 Agile allows each project team to select the tools and communication processes that are best suited to the needs of the team members – and to adjust the tools as the project progresses to meet their ongoing needs. The following questions will help you to determine the right tools for your project:

Chapter 5: Moving From PRINCE2 to PRINCE2 Agile

- What tools are the project delivery team members planning to use in support of their own work (e.g. backlogs, Kanban boards)?
- Are these tools accessible to the project manager and the Project Board? If not, could they be made accessible with minimal additional effort by the project delivery team?
- Do these tools provide the project manager and Project Board with the ongoing status, quality, issue, risk, and configuration management information that they need? If not, what could be added to provide the additional detail without requiring a substantial amount of extra work for the project delivery team?
- How does the Project Board want to be notified of status information, issues, and risks? Are they happy to have this information available for their access (i.e. "pulling" the information) or would they prefer the information to be prepared and presented to them (i.e. "pushing" the information)? Note that, if the Project Board wants the information pushed to them, this would generally be the responsibility of the project manager, with support from the team manager as required.

The answers to these questions will also help the project manager determine what additional tools are needed to support PRINCE2 Agile reporting requirements.

It is worth noting that Project Board members are likely to request access to more information at the start of the project than they will continue to need as the project progresses (particularly if they are new to PRINCE2 Agile and hesitant about fully empowering the project delivery team). It is recommended that the project team members do not spend substantial time at the start of the project creating additional tools that may have limited value over the project timeline. It may be more beneficial for the project manager to temporarily provide the additional communication that the Project Board is requesting as a manual exercise (i.e. asking team members for updates) than to create an extensive range of registers,

Chapter 5: Moving From PRINCE2 to PRINCE2 Agile

spreadsheets, etc. that may not be needed after the first few iterations/releases.

Step 6: Identify management strategies and project controls

The communication and reporting tools identified in the previous step provide the foundation for the project team to manage status, quality, configuration items, issues, and risks as part of ongoing project work. To ensure the effective governance of the project work in accordance with PRINCE2 requirements, the project also needs to establish formal strategies that identify how these tools (and other processes) will be used to manage these critical project areas, specifically:

- a communication management strategy
- a configuration management strategy
- a quality management strategy and
- a risk management strategy.

The team should try, wherever possible, to leverage the tools identified in Step 5 in these strategies to minimize the need for additional work, e.g. using information radiators as the primary issue communication tool within the project delivery team and escalating significant issues in a separate issues register.

The Project Board and project manager will also need to identify whether additional tools will be required to provide highlight reporting, checkpoint reporting, exception reporting, and end stage reporting – and to what extent the existing tools can satisfy these requirements.

In addition to establishing formal strategies to manage key project areas, the Project Board will also need to identify the acceptable *tolerances* for reporting on variations in Benefits, Scope, Time, Cost, Quality, and Risk as the project progresses. As described in *Chapter 3: Overview of PRINCE2 Agile*, PRINCE2 Agile focuses on having *flexible* Scope and Quality variables, *possibly flexible* Benefits and Risk variables, and *fixed* Time and Cost variables. Therefore it is reasonable to assume that Scope and Quality would have higher tolerances

Chapter 5: Moving From PRINCE2 to PRINCE2 Agile

(i.e. allowing for more variation before reporting is required) and that Time and Cost would have much lower or zero tolerances (i.e. any variation on these would need to be reported to the Project Board). The Project Board's familiarity in using PRINCE2 Agile can also influence their decision on how much variation they can allow for, with the potential for originally set tolerances to be increased as the project matures and the Project Board becomes more comfortable with this approach.

Step 7: Get approval for the baseline PID

At this point in the planning process, the project will have:

- an identified project team
- a shared vision of the outcomes and outputs that the project is expected to deliver
- the intended timelines for delivery
- an understanding of the tools that are available (or need to be developed) to monitor and manage ongoing project work and
- agreed project controls.

You are now in a position to create the baseline PID for Project Board review and approval for the project work to begin (or to refine the PID that you have been working on at each step).

In PRINCE2 Agile, the PID can be as formal or informal as the Project Board and project manager require. Where possible, the tools and processes identified in the previous steps should be used in lieu of including (and maintaining) substantial project management information within the PID itself. This will minimize the need for significant and frequent updates to the PID as the project progresses.

It is important to remember that the PID is being developed as a *baseline* document that is intended to be used as a starting point and adapted as the project progresses to reflect emergent information.

Chapter 5: Moving From PRINCE2 to PRINCE2 Agile

During this time, the project manager may also need to update the other supporting documentation for project approval, including the business case (as needed), the benefits review plan, and the project product description.

Step 8: Start the project work

When the Project Board has approved the PID, the project manager can develop the stage plan and work package(s) for the first stage of the project. This is where the project focus shifts from *planning* to *execution*, with the selected Agile method driving the production of outputs in accordance with the agreed plan.

For the project delivery team, this is the first iteration of Agile work based on the top-down priorities identified in the product backlog (and may include the Discovery Phase for initial investigation work, as determined in the release planning in Step 4 above). This would be the first of several iterations leading to one or more releases which fulfill the requirements of the first stage. (Further detail on how to use the selected Agile method for effective project delivery is provided in the *Bibliography*.)

It is important for the project manager to ensure that the stage plan for this work is written in a way that supports the use of Agile tools and agreed processes wherever possible, e.g. by having the project product description detail refer out to the product backlog instead of replicating its contents within the document (and needing to update it throughout the stage).

Similarly, the work packages for this stage need to be written in a way that allows the Agile method to manage ongoing work without creating a significant documentation overhead for the team.

The intent is to ensure that the primary focus of the project delivery team is on producing the required outputs, with governance and oversight occurring as a natural extension of the tools that the team is already using.

Chapter 5: Moving From PRINCE2 to PRINCE2 Agile

Step 9: Monitor the project work

As the project work progresses in each stage, the project delivery team uses the agreed Agile method to build the highest-priority capabilities within the allocated timeframes for the work packages identified in the release plan.[38]

Within each stage, the project manager has ongoing responsibility for overseeing project progress, facilitating project work, getting required approvals, managing project tolerances, addressing exceptions, maintaining project records, and communicating with the Project Board through highlight reports and at other times as needed.

The team manager supports the project manager by managing the work packages being delivered by the team and updating the project manager on the progress of their work (where the team manager is a separate role).

Ongoing project status, issue, and risk information throughout the stage is made available to the project manager and Project Board using the communication tools agreed in Step 5.

At each review, the product owner(s), and other CSMEs, product specialists, etc., have the opportunity to confirm whether the outputs that the project delivery team has produced in that timeframe meet their expectations, and adjust ongoing work accordingly.

At each stage review, the senior user(s) have the opportunity to assess whether the capabilities that the project delivery team has produced across all of the iterations/releases in that stage are generating the anticipated level of business value and meeting their quality expectations in order to approve progressing to the next stage. Note that the involvement of the

---

[38] The resources on the project delivery team should remain consistent throughout the project (i.e. across all stages) wherever possible to maximize the value of their Agile work and the accuracy of Agile metrics, e.g. velocity.

Chapter 5: Moving From PRINCE2 to PRINCE2 Agile

senior user can occur more frequently, e.g. at iteration reviews, as determined by the communication channels established for the project.

At each review point, it is important that the project team include *retrospectives*, reviewing both the effectiveness of the Agile method used *and* the PRINCE2 Agile governance structure. (These may be conducted as sprint reviews in Scrum or as service delivery/operations reviews in Kanban.) These review sessions should include comparisons of baseline versus actual measurements, and reviews of benefits achieved, issues encountered, and lessons learned. Where needed, the project team should endeavor to refine these approaches *as the project progresses*, instead of waiting for the stage end or project closure.

These review sessions can also include:

- Conducting a PRINCE2 Agile Health Check using the checklists that are provided in Appendix C of the AXELOS official guide.
- Using the Stoplight Reporting tool in Section 7.5 of the AXELOS official guide to determine whether the key PRINCE2 Agile principles are being adhered to – and to raise an exception if they are not.

Both of these tools are specifically designed for the monitoring and refinement of PRINCE2 Agile work.

Project work continues within the iterations/releases agreed for each approved stage until the project is closed, as described in the following step.

Step 10: Close the project

There will be a point where the project work will naturally (or unexpectedly) come to an end, because of one of the following:

- All of the intended outcomes have been achieved (including capabilities that have been released into a live environment where they can be measured).

Chapter 5: Moving From PRINCE2 to PRINCE2 Agile

- The project is not delivering the level of business value that was expected.
- The remaining work for the project does not deliver sufficient business value to justify the project continuing (particularly likely where Agile methods have focused on delivering the highest business-value outputs first).
- The project needs to be ended unexpectedly due to changes in the organization, budget availability, market conditions, etc. (even if the project work was delivering its intended outcomes).

For all of these scenarios, PRINCE2 Agile has a structured approach to project closure that should be followed, as detailed in Section 4.3 of the AXELOS official guide.

Importantly, the use of Agile methods, high communication, and transparency throughout project delivery means that project closure is generally more of a clean-up activity where the Project Board is already aware of:

- what outputs have (and have not) been produced
- whether the outputs produced meet the acceptance criteria (or allowed tolerances within these criteria)
- how well the outputs produced align with the expected benefits
- what issues and risks the project team encountered (and which of these have not yet been resolved)
- whether there were any unexpected project costs.

Ideally, this means that there should be no surprises at this point in the process. The primary focus for the project team will be to:

- Hold a project retrospective that focuses on reviewing the effectiveness of the PRINCE2 Agile framework, comparing baseline versus actual measurements, and documenting lessons learned for future project work (including decisions on the ongoing use of Agile methods).

Chapter 5: Moving From PRINCE2 to PRINCE2 Agile

- Finalize any remaining PRINCE2 Agile documentation (generally done by the project manager with support from the team manager and other team members as required).
- Implement any methods or tools that will be needed to measure the value of released capabilities (as described in the benefits review plan) after the project is closed.

This step should also include formal confirmation from the senior user(s) on the extent to which the requirements of the original business case have been met.

The documentation produced for project closure will serve as a formal record of what the project did (and did not) achieve and, equally important, as a learning tool for future PRINCE2 Agile teams.

CHAPTER 6: MERGING EXISTING PRINCE2 AND AGILE METHODS

The previous section identified the required steps for implementing PRINCE2 Agile by introducing Agile methods into your *existing* PRINCE2 structure. The approach that was described is ideal for those organizations that have an established PRINCE2 framework with project work traditionally being delivered using waterfall approaches. It is quite possible, however, for PRINCE2 organizations to already have project teams that have been delivering outputs using Agile methods, where the two approaches have been working *in parallel* instead of using an *integrated* approach like PRINCE2 Agile.

This includes both situations where the use of Agile methods was explicitly known to the management team, and situations where the decision to use Agile methods was made independently by the project delivery team, even though it had not yet been officially endorsed by the organization (otherwise known as "Agile by stealth").

If you are implementing PRINCE2 Agile in a PRINCE2 organization that already has project teams using Agile methods (whether or not they were officially endorsed by senior management), this presents both opportunities and challenges for the project work. In most cases, these teams will not have definitive metrics for the work that they have done to date. They are, however, likely to have a number of work products, including Agile communication tools, delivered software, and customer testimonials, which can indicate how well their employed Agile approaches worked. They are also likely to have acquired a substantial amount of knowledge about what does – and does not – work within your organizational culture. All of this information can be applied to selecting the best ongoing approaches for your department to

Chapter 6: Merging Existing PRINCE2 and Agile Methods

use and the expansion of the project team's Agile work – now with the benefit of your support.

In this project scenario, the project team can primarily use the 10 steps identified in *Chapter 5: Moving from PRINCE2 to PRINCE2 Agile* implement their PRINCE2 Agile work with one key activity added at the beginning of the process.

Step 0: Take a pulse point

To fully understand how to integrate your existing PRINCE2 and Agile methods into a cohesive PRINCE2 Agile framework, it is important to know what Agile methods and practices the project delivery team members have been using and how successful (or challenging) these approaches have been.

For example, the project delivery team may have been using Scrum on their own initiative to time-box their work, increase team communication, and focus on delivering the highest-priority features identified by the business.

In their use of Scrum, the delivery team members may have also taken the initiative to establish high-communication channels within the team, such as visible information radiators, face-to-face meetings (instead of numerous back-and-forth emails), and daily stand-up meetings to check in with each other where possible. These are practices that can be leveraged for use in the PRINCE2 Agile framework with minimal overheads and training. It is a "quick win" for the project team.

On the other hand, the delivery team members may have also made arrangements with one or more of their preferred business users to work with the team as "unofficial" customer representatives to clarify and refine their ongoing work. This presents both an opportunity and a challenge in the PRINCE2 Agile framework. It is a positive sign that the project delivery team appreciates the importance of business user input enough to seek it out; however, the value of the input that they have been receiving is contingent upon the capabilities and knowledge of their selected user(s), who may only represent specific business areas – or who may not be senior enough to provide strategic or visionary feedback to the team.

Chapter 6: Merging Existing PRINCE2 and Agile Methods

In the PRINCE2 Agile framework, the Project Board and the project manager are responsible for deciding who is in the best position to represent the business requirements for the organization, and assigning them as the product owner(s) for the project, even if the selected person does not have as much hands-on knowledge or history – or availability – as the user(s) who were previously selected by the team. This does not stop the project delivery team from arranging with their preferred users to act as business ambassadors; it does, however, mean that they will need to negotiate for this, where they had been the sole decision-makers before. It also means that the project delivery team members and the selected business ambassadors will need to defer to the officially nominated product owner in product decisions.

This is one situation where existing standalone Agile methods can be both a benefit and a hurdle in an integrated PRINCE2 Agile structure. Project delivery team members will have the experience and knowledge of Agile methods (and possibly the formal certification) which allows them to start project work much more quickly. This experience also provides them with lessons learned on previous projects to make them more efficient. They also, however, may have worked in environments where the project delivery team had the sole authority to make decisions, and they need to adjust this mindset to align with the PRINCE2 Agile governance model.

Once the project team has an understanding of the Agile methods that are already in use within the organization – and their effectiveness – the project can proceed with Steps 1 to 10 as detailed in the previous chapter.

CHAPTER 7: MOVING AN EXISTING WATERFALL PROJECT TO PRINCE2 AGILE

If you have an existing project that has been delivered using waterfall methods and you want to transition the project (or subsequent stages of the project) to PRINCE2 Agile, there are two different approaches to use, depending on whether or not the existing project has been delivered within a PRINCE2 framework.

If your existing waterfall project uses PRINCE2

If the existing project already has a PRINCE2 framework, it is recommended that you use the steps detailed in *Chapter 5: Moving from PRINCE2 to PRINCE2 Agile* with the following variations:

Step 0: Take a pulse point

For an existing waterfall project, this is an opportunity to review what work has been produced by the team, including previous outputs, outstanding requirements, documentation, and lessons learned.

As these project artifacts will most likely align with PRINCE2 requirements, they could theoretically be used as the baseline for developing equivalent PRINCE2 Agile project documentation; however, it may be more valuable to consider them good sources of *historical information*, and to create new project documents that are fully compliant with the structure and principles of PRINCE2 Agile moving forward, as described in the following steps.

Step 1: Identify the right project team

In this situation, the Project Board members will have most likely already been identified. The key is to identify the project

Chapter 7: Moving an Existing Waterfall Project to PRINCE2 Agile

delivery team that can support the selected Agile delivery method. This may be the existing project team (especially if they have intimate knowledge of existing deliverables) with the appropriate Agile training.

Step 2: Establish a shared vision

This would be approached in the same way as moving any team to a PRINCE2 Agile model as described in *Chapter 5: Moving from PRINCE2 to PRINCE2 Agile*.

Step 3: Define the outcomes and outputs

This would be approached in the same way as moving any team to a PRINCE2 Agile model, with the exception that there may be existing requirements documents that need to be transitioned to be PRINCE2 Agile artifacts (e.g. turning detailed specification documents into user stories and prioritizing them in a product backlog).

Step 4: Define the release plan

This would be approached in the same way as moving any team to a PRINCE2 Agile model, with the caveat that referring to previously produced waterfall project plans could actually prove to be a *disservice* to the PRINCE2 Agile project planning. It is better for the project team to extract any known milestone dates from the waterfall project plan as input into ongoing PRINCE2 Agile planning – and then break away completely from the previous plan in favor of the responsive Agile planning model.

Step 5: Define the tolerances

This would be approached in the same way as moving any team to a PRINCE2 Agile model.

Chapter 7: Moving an Existing Waterfall Project to PRINCE2 Agile

Step 6: Choose your tools

This would be approached in the same way as moving any team to a PRINCE2 Agile model.

Step 7: Get approval for the baseline PID

This would be approached in the same way as moving any team to a PRINCE2 Agile model, with the caveat that referring to the previously produced waterfall PID could also be a *disservice* to the PRINCE2 Agile project planning. Similar to Step 4, it is better for the project team to extract any critical information from previously produced PID(s) and other project planning documents, and then archive them as historical documents.

Step 8: Start the project work

This would be approached in the same way as moving any team to a PRINCE2 Agile model.

Step 9: Monitor the project work

This would be approached in the same way as moving any team to a PRINCE2 Agile model.

Step 10: Close the project

This would be approached in the same way as moving any team to a PRINCE2 Agile model, with the exception that the project documentation may need to include both the historical waterfall artifacts and the PRINCE2 Agile artifacts.

If your existing waterfall project uses a different governance structure (or no formal governance structure)

If your existing waterfall project does not already have a PRINCE2 framework, it is recommended that you use the steps detailed in *Chapter 8: Implementing PRINCE2 Agile with No*

Chapter 7: Moving an Existing Waterfall Project to PRINCE2 Agile

Existing Framework, with any existing waterfall project documentation being used only as information sources and then archived.

CHAPTER 8: IMPLEMENTING PRINCE2 AGILE WITH NO EXISTING FRAMEWORK

The previous three sections focused on project situations that *existing* PRINCE2 organizations are likely to encounter in their transition to PRINCE2 Agile. In all of these sections, it was assumed that staff had the necessary training, certification, and experience to successfully deliver PRINCE2 projects – and that the implementation of PRINCE2 Agile was an *expansion* of their existing knowledge.

There are, however, other project situations that organizations may encounter if they are interested in implementing a PRINCE2 Agile framework and they *do not* have the benefit of an existing PRINCE2 framework to work from. This includes:

- Organizations that have no existing governance or project management framework *and* no experience in using Agile methods.
- Organizations that have no existing governance or project management framework, but they do have the benefit of project teams that are experienced in using Agile methods.

This section addresses the first of these situations to guide those organizations that have no existing governance framework to leverage *and* no experience in using Agile methods.

The next chapter, *Chapter 9: Moving from Agile to PRINCE2 Agile*, is for organizations that have experience with Agile methods and want to leverage that experience in their transition to PRINCE2 Agile.

For organizations with no existing governance framework or experience with Agile methods, implementing a *wholly new project* using PRINCE2 Agile is, in many respects, the easiest and most efficient way to implement this method. You are not saddled with incorporating legacy artifacts (e.g. waterfall

Chapter 8: Implementing PRINCE2 Agile with No Existing Framework

project plans) into your PRINCE2 Agile project; you do not need staff to "unlearn" previously established frameworks, processes, and behaviors; and you are less likely to encounter resistance from project team members who are used to working on projects in a particular way.

On the other hand, a wholly new PRINCE2 Agile framework will require training staff and establishing new project structures, and will have limited historical information to leverage.

The most important thing to remember is that PRINCE2 Agile is a *supplement to* – and *not a substitute for* – the proper implementation of PRINCE2. Therefore the first step is for the organization to establish a viable PRINCE2 framework for portfolio, program, and project management before endeavoring to implement PRINCE2 Agile.

Once the PRINCE2 framework is in place, it can be transitioned to PRINCE2 Agile using the step-by-step approach described in *Chapter 5: Moving from PRINCE2 to PRINCE2 Agile*.

At first glance, this may seem like a substantial commitment of time, budget, and resources to obtain the benefits of PRINCE2 Agile for your project, but it really should be viewed as an investment in your organization to more effectively deliver all of your projects moving forward.

CHAPTER 9: MOVING FROM AGILE TO PRINCE2 AGILE

As mentioned in the previous section, there are organizations that may be interested in implementing a PRINCE2 Agile framework to provide a governance structure around their current Agile project work. This is particularly true for organizations that want to combine the effectiveness of their existing Agile delivery approaches with the *adaptive governance* and *ongoing business-value confirmation from management* that PRINCE2 Agile provides.

Although it may seem unlikely that senior management would institute a governance framework around a project delivery method, it is not unprecedented. In fact, the success of Agile methods has been known to inspire senior management to institute organization-wide changes. (This is exactly what occurred at BT.[39])

As in the previous section, the important thing to remember is that PRINCE2 Agile is a *supplement to* – and *not a substitute for* – the proper implementation of PRINCE2.

As implementing the PRINCE2 Agile framework can be a substantial commitment for senior management, it is worthwhile for the organization to take a step back and consider *why* this decision is being made, particularly if your Agile teams are already achieving required outcomes without a formalized project management and governance framework (i.e. "if it ain't broke, don't fix it").

---

[39] L. Meadows and S. Hanly, *Agile Coaching in British Telecom* (2006), www.agileconnection.com/article/agile-coaching-british-telecom.

Chapter 9: Moving From Agile to PRINCE2 Agile

Is senior management introducing governance and project management structures because they are concerned that their Agile projects are outside of management control? Are they being introduced to fulfill a compliance mandate or a customer requirement?

The AXELOS official guide recommends that existing Agile organizations consider situations where mature Agile methods are already in place to determine whether PRINCE2 Agile will provide substantial benefits over the current model. It advises that PRINCE2 Agile may be appropriate to provide governance for a more challenging project, or to align Agile work with existing PRINCE2 or PRINCE2 Agile teams. However, it equally advises that organizations may want to consider alternative methods to achieve these outcomes.[40]

If your organization does decide to transition your current Agile work to the PRINCE2 Agile framework, the first step is for the organization to establish a viable PRINCE2 framework for portfolio, program, and project management before endeavoring to implement PRINCE2 Agile.

Once the PRINCE2 framework is in place, it can be transitioned to PRINCE2 Agile using the approach described in *Chapter 6: Merging Existing PRINCE2 and Agile Methods*.

If your organization does proceed with this approach, it would be beneficial for you to publish a case study about your experience in transitioning from Agile to PRINCE2 Agile to encourage other Agile organizations to do the same thing.

---

[40] Section 3.3, *PRINCE2 Agile*, Keith Richards, AXELOS (2015): *www.axelos.com/store/book/prince2-agile*.

CHAPTER 10: FURTHER EXPANSION OF PRINCE2 AGILE

All of the PRINCE2 Agile descriptions throughout this book refer specifically to *project* work, i.e. project delivery, project teams, project stages. This is based on the understanding that the work in an organization can generally be divided into two categories:

1. The *business-as-usual* (BAU) activities that are the ongoing operational tasks for the organization, such as manufacturing, customer support, sales, human resources.
2. The *project* activities that are temporary groupings of staff to deliver specific business outcomes, generally within a fixed timeframe and budget.

The PRINCE2 Agile framework in the AXELOS official guide is intended for *project* work, where there is an official starting point (i.e. project initiation), review opportunities as the project is progressing (i.e. iterations, releases, and stages), and an official point of completion (i.e. project closure), with the project outputs, as appropriate, transitioning to BAU activities.

Chapter 10: Further Expansion of PRINCE2 Agile

There is, however, potential for organizations to structure their BAU activities to function as project work,[41] for example:

- Treat the start of each financial year as the start of a year-long BAU project with the project objectives being the delivery of agreed metrics, such as increased sales, reduced operational costs, higher employee retention rates, greater levels of customer satisfaction.
- Subdivide the BAU work over the course of the year into time-based stages, e.g. monthly, quarterly.
- Manage the ongoing BAU work within each stage using Kanban, Lean, Scrumban or equivalent Agile methods intended to optimize production activities.
- Treat the end of the financial year as the project closure, with confirmation of intended objectives, documentation of outcomes, and preparation for the next year-long BAU project in the upcoming financial year.

With this approach, organizations can leverage PRINCE2 Agile to achieve integrated governance and delivery efficiencies in their BAU work at an equivalent value to what PRINCE2 Agile provides for project work.

---

[41] Where senior management should determine whether the overheads required to manage this work in the PRINCE2 Agile framework justify the business value achieved.

BIBLIOGRAPHY

The following are PRINCE2, Agile and PRINCE2 Agile sources that you can refer to for further information

PRINCE2 resources

PRINCE2: *www.axelos.com/best-practice-solutions/prince2*

PRINCE2.com: *www.prince2.com/usa*

PRINCE2 Agile resources

PRINCE2 Agile, Keith Richards, AXELOS (2015): *www.axelos.com/store/book/prince2-agile*

Taking Agile to PRINCE2, Raconteur (2015), *http://raconteur.net/business/taking-agile-to-prince2*

General information on Agile

Agile Alliance: *www.agilealliance.com*

Agile: An Executive Guide – Real Results from IT Budgets, Jamie Lynn Cooke, IT Governance Publishing (2011): *www.itgovernanceusa.com/shop/p-351-Agile-an-executive-guide.aspx#.uc7geqwlfg0*

Agile Connection: *www.agileconnection.com*

AgileKiwi: Practical Agile software development: *www.agilekiwi.com*

Agile Manifesto: *www.agilemanifesto.org*

AgileSoftwareDevelopment.com: *www.agilesoftwaredevelopment.com*

Alistair Cockburn: *http://alistair.cockburn.us*

Bibliography

Everything You Want to Know about Agile, Jamie Lynn Cooke, IT Governance Publishing (2012): *www.itgovernanceusa.com/shop/p-549-everything-youwant-to-know-about-Agile.aspx*

The Power of the Agile Business Analyst: 30 Surprising Ways a Business Analyst Can Add Value to Your Agile Development Team, Jamie Lynn Cooke, IT Governance Publishing (2013): *www.itgovernanceusa.com/shop/p-1379-the-power-of-the-agile-business-analyst.aspx*

Specific Agile methods

Overview

A Practical Guide to Seven Agile Methodologies, R. Coffin and D. Lane: Part One: *www.devx.com/architect/article/32761*;

Part Two: *www.devx.com/architect/article/32836*

Scrum

Scrum alliance: *www.scrumalliance.org*

Glossary of Scrum Terms, V. Szalvay, Scrum Alliance, Inc. (2007): *www.scrumalliance.org/community/articles/2007/march/glossary-of-scrum-terms*

Scrum and Agile presentations by Mike Cohn of Mountain Goat Software (various dates): *www.mountaingoatsoftware.com/presentations*

DSDM

What Is DSDM?, M. Clifton and J. Dunlap (2003): *www.codeproject.com/kb/architecture/dsdm.aspx*

DSDM Explained, R. Davies, JAOO (2004): *www.agilexp.com/presentations/DSDMexplained.pdf*

Bibliography

FDD™

Feature-Driven Development: An Overview: *www.tarrani.net/mike/docs/fddoverview.pdf*

Feature-Driven Development™ (FDD™) and Agile Modeling, S.W. Ambler: *www.agilemodeling.com/essays/fdd.htm*

Lean

Lean Primer, C. Larman and B. Vodde (2009): *www.leanprimer.com/downloads/lean_primer.pdf*

Leading Lean Software Development: Results Are Not the Point, Poppendieck LLC (2009): *www.poppendieck.com/pdfs/llsd_intro.pdf*

XP™

eXtreme Programming™: A Gentle Introduction: *www.extremeprogramming.org*

Kanban and Scrumban

Kanban (overview): *www.crisp.se/kanban*

Kanban and Scrum: Making the Most of Both, H. Kniberg and M. Skarin (2010): *www.infoq.com/minibooks/kanban-scrum-minibook*

Scrum-ban: *http://leansoftwareengineering.com/ksse/scrum-ban/*

Scrumban: Essays on Kanban Systems for Lean Software Development, C. Ladas, Modus Cooperandi Press (2009)

Scrumban: Taking Scrum Outside Its Comfort Zone: *www.slideshare.net/yyeret/scrumban-taking-scrum-outside-its-comfort-zone*

Bibliography

RUP®

What Is the Rational Unified Process®:
www.ibm.com/developerworks/rational/library/content/Rationa lEdge/jan01/WhatIstheRationalUnifiedProcessJan01.pdf

Agile Modeling and the Rational Unified Process® (RUP®):
www.agilemodeling.com/ essays/Agilemodelingrup.htm

AUP

The Agile Unified Process (AUP): www.ambysoft.com/ unifiedprocess/Agileup.html

Crystal

Crystal methodologies:
http://alistair.cockburn.us/crystal+methodologies

Scaled Agile Framework® (SAFe®)

Scaled Agile Framework® (SAFe®):
www.scaledagileframework.com

Introducing the Scaled Agile Framework®:
www.cio.com/article/2936942/enterprise-software/introducing-the-scaled-agile-framework.html

Large-Scale Scrum (LeSS) Framework

Introduction to LeSS:
http://less.works/less/framework/introduction.html

Nexus

Nexus Framework: www.scrum.org/Resources/The-Nexus-Guide

Scrum of Scrums

Agile Can Scale: Inventing and Reinventing SCRUM in Five Companies: *www.controlchaos.com/storage/scrum-articles/Sutherland%20200111%20proof.pdf*

Disciplined Agile Delivery (DAD)

The Disciplined Agile Framework: *www.disciplinedagiledelivery.com/agility-at-scale/disciplined-agile-2/*

Industry research on Agile

9th Annual State of Agile Development Survey, VersionOne: *http://info.versionone.com/state-of-agile-development-survey-ninth.html*

Selected Agile case studies

Agile Coaching in British Telecom, L. Meadows and S. Hanly (2006): *www.agilejournal.com/articles/columns/column-articles/144-agile-coaching-in-british-telecom*

Rolling Out Agile in a Large Enterprise, G. Benefield Proceedings of the 41st Annual Hawaii International Conference on System Sciences (HICSS) (2008): *http://dl.acm.org/citation.cfm?id=1334591*

ITG RESOURCES

IT Governance Ltd sources, creates and delivers products and services to meet the real-world, evolving IT governance needs of today's organisations, directors, managers and practitioners.

The ITG website (*www.itgovernance.co.uk*) is the international one-stop-shop for corporate and IT governance information, advice, guidance, books, tools, training and consultancy. On the website you will find the following page related to the subject matter of this book:

www.itgovernance.co.uk/project_governance.aspx.

Publishing Services

IT Governance Publishing (ITGP) is the world's leading IT-GRC publishing imprint that is wholly owned by IT Governance Ltd.

With books and tools covering all IT governance, risk and compliance frameworks, we are the publisher of choice for authors and distributors alike, producing unique and practical publications of the highest quality, in the latest formats available, which readers will find invaluable.

www.itgovernancepublishing.co.uk is the website dedicated to ITGP. Other titles published by ITGP that may be of interest include:

- The Power of the Agile Business Analyst
  www.itgovernance.co.uk/shop/p-1457.aspx

- Everything you want to know about Agile
  www.itgovernance.co.uk/shop/p-549.aspx

- The Concise PRINCE2
  www.itgovernance.co.uk/shop/p-1165.aspx

ITG Resources

We also offer a range of off-the-shelf toolkits that give comprehensive, customisable documents to help users create the specific documentation they need to properly implement a management system or standard. Written by experienced practitioners and based on the latest best practice, ITGP toolkits can save months of work for organisations working towards compliance with a given standard.

Please visit *www.itgovernance.co.uk/shop/c-129-toolkits.aspx* to see our full range of toolkits.

Books and tools published by IT Governance Publishing (ITGP) are available from all business booksellers and the following websites:

www.itgovernance.eu   *www.itgovernanceusa.com*

www.itgovernance.in   *www.itgovernancesa.co.za*

www.itgovernance.asia.

Training Services

IT Governance offers an extensive portfolio of training courses designed to educate information security, IT governance, risk management and compliance professionals. Our classroom and online training programmes will help you develop the skills required to deliver best practice and compliance to your organisation. They will also enhance your career by providing you with industry standard certifications and increased peer recognition. Our range of courses offer a structured learning path from Foundation to Advanced level in the key topics of information security, IT governance, business continuity and service management.

Full details of all IT Governance training courses can be found at *www.itgovernance.co.uk/training.aspx*.

Professional Services and Consultancy

The IT Governance Professional Services team can show you how to apply Agile concepts to the most complex development projects. Our expert consultants can guide and inspire you in the use of Agile, providing you with the practical techniques to improve delivery efficiencies, control your implementation costs, and meet your sales targets by building customer loyalty.

We will show you the Agile methods that create flexibility and ensure adaptability to changing circumstances, accepting that nothing changes more than your customer's needs. You will learn how to change from a traditional hierarchy towards self-empowered individuals and teams. In this way, you will develop engaged employees with the responsibility, accountability and authority to deliver to the customer's requirements, shaping and directing outcomes, while regularly delivering partial, though functional, products.

For more information about IT Governance: Consultancy and Training Services see:

www.itgovernance.co.uk/consulting.aspx.

Newsletter

You can stay up to date with the latest developments across the whole spectrum of IT governance subject matter, including risk management, information security, ITIL and IT service management, project governance, compliance and so much more, by subscribing to our newsletter.

Simply visit our subscription centre and select your preferences:

www.itgovernance.co.uk/newsletter.aspx.

Lightning Source UK Ltd.
Milton Keynes UK
UKOW06f0804060916

282323UK00016B/232/P